TENNIS
AND THE
NEWPORT CASINO

TENNIS
AND THE
NEWPORT CASINO

*International Tennis
Hall of Fame
& Museum*

ARCADIA
PUBLISHING

Published by Arcadia Publishing
Charleston, South Carolina

Library of Congress Control Number: 2010938692

For all general information, please contact Arcadia Publishing:
Telephone 843-853-2070
Fax 843-853-0044
E-mail sales@arcadiapublishing.com
For customer service and orders:
Toll-Free 1-888-313-2665

Visit us on the Internet at www.arcadiapublishing.com

*In memory of all those individuals who have made the Newport Casino
one of the world's finest destinations.*

CONTENTS

ACKNOWLEDGMENTS

Tennis and the Newport Casino represents the first book highlighting the International Tennis Hall of Fame & Museum's collection. The museum is home to one of the world's finest repositories devoted to the history of tennis, the Newport Casino, and the sport's impact on our culture. Our museum chronicles the history of tennis and Gilded Age Newport from the 14th century to the present in 18 galleries covering more than 12,000 square feet of exhibition space.

Photographs used in this book are part of the museum's collection. The museum has more than 350,000 images that were consulted for this book. The images include those taken or provided by *American Lawn Tennis*; Avery Library, Columbia University; Michael Baz; William Burgin; John Corbett; Cullen Designs; Edward Fernberger; Kim Fuller; Heidi Gumula, of Durkee, Brown, Viveiros and Werenfels (DBVW) Architects; Max Peter Haas; Craig Harris; Historic Alman Photographers; the family of Dr. Robert Johnson; Paule Loring; Kathryn Whitney Lucey; Cailin Mateleska; Patrick McMullen; *Newport Daily News*; Newport Historical Society; Wendy Parks; Lloyd Pauley; Philip Morris Company; Jennifer Pottheiser; Greg Premru; Rotofoto, Inc.; Rowland Scherman/Hulton Archive/Getty Images; Wide World Photo; and *World Tennis*. Unless otherwise noted, all photographs are courtesy of the International Tennis Hall of Fame & Museum, Newport, Rhode Island.

The museum has a rich history from its founding in 1954 to the present. Its success today represents the collective effort of many individuals whose tireless work to collect, preserve, interpret, educate, promote, champion, and raise supporting funds has made the museum one of Newport's finest attractions. Special thanks go to Jefferson T. Barnes, Jane Brown Grimes, Joseph F. Cullman III, John Davis, Marilyn and Edward Fernberger, Jan Leschly, Col. Fred Long, Alastair Martin, William McChesney Martin, John Reese, Mark Stenning, Jimmy and Candy Van Alen, Rosalind P. Walter, and Peggy and Edgar Woolard. Without their commitment and dedication over the years, the museum would not be what it is today.

The museum staff is pleased to present this book and hopes that it provides you with a greater understanding and deeper appreciation of one of the world's best sports museums and historic complexes.

INTRODUCTION

Since its grand opening in the summer of 1880, the Newport Casino has been an integral and timeless component of the social and cultural fabric of Newport, Rhode Island. Commissioned by James Gordon Bennett, the publisher of the *New York Herald*, and designed by the renowned architectural firm of McKim, Mead & White, the Casino is a masterpiece of Victorian elegance, complete with shingled towers and latticed porches. Its opening heralded a new era in Newport society. From the late 1880s through the 1920s, the Newport Casino was a place for recreation and included concerts, dancing, dining, horse shows, lawn bowling, tea parties, and theatricals, along with its present-day offerings of lawn and court tennis.

The birth of American tournament tennis began in 1881 when the Casino hosted the first U.S. National Championships, the forerunner of the US Open, and annually thereafter through 1914. Tournament tennis has been played here ever since, including the present-day Hall of Fame Tennis Championships, an event on the ATP World Tour. Each July, Tennis Week in Newport allows fans to experience top-flight tennis.

Since that first championship in 1881, the world's best players have competed in Newport, the cradle of American tennis. Dick Sears, Dwight Davis, Bill Tilden, Don Budge, Tony Trabert, Rod Laver, Margaret Court, Billie Jean King, Chris Evert, John McEnroe, Jim Courier, and Arantxa Sánchez-Vicario represent just a handful of the more than 100 Hall of Famers who have played on our grass courts. These courts are the world's oldest continuously used competition grass courts, which are available for public play in the summer.

The International Tennis Hall of Fame & Museum was established in 1954. A year later, the first of more than 200 Hall of Famers were inducted in what has become an annual Newport tradition. A National Historic Landmark, the Newport Casino houses one of the world's finest museums devoted to the sport of tennis and the history of the Casino. The complex also has a facility for court tennis, the sport from which tennis evolved, which is one of the few remaining court tennis facilities in the United States. In addition, the site hosts the opening nights of the Newport Folk Festival and Jazz Festival, two of New England's most accomplished musical events. Jazz greats such as Bill Davidson, Billie Holiday, Dizzy Gillespie, Ella Fitzgerald, Harry Connick Jr., Diana Krall, and Tony Bennett have all performed at the Newport Casino, while music icon Bob Dylan graced our lawns with his presence at the Newport Folk Festival from 1963 to 1965.

Finally, the renovation and restoration of the Casino Theatre, original to the site and the last surviving Stanford White theater anywhere, completes the property. This long-standing project was completed in 2010. The beautiful Casino Theatre, which hosted plays, performances, and theatricals, from Orson Welles and Vincent Price to Eva Gabor, Ray Parker, and Mary Astor, will again be the site of great Newport theater.

We release *Tennis and the Newport Casino* as we celebrate two major milestones in our history. First, 2010 marked the 130th anniversary of the opening of the Newport Casino. Secondly, 2011 is the 130th anniversary of the first U.S. National Championships held at the Newport Casino in 1881. Interspersed among these celebrations is the reopening of the Casino Theatre. This allows us to celebrate our history and reaffirm our relationship to the Newport community.

1

THE NEWPORT CASINO

Home to the International Tennis Hall of Fame & Museum, the Newport Casino is an integral part of Newport's rich architectural and cultural history. Conceptualized, designed, and built in under a year, this jewel was the "sporting mansion," or clubhouse, for Newport's summer elite, yet its concept was unique by welcoming the public with numerous activities on the grounds.

Commissioned by summer resident James Gordon Bennett following an incident of boyish entertainment gone awry at the Newport Reading Room, this popular social club brought sporting activities to the forefront. Bennett hired the newly formed architectural firm of McKim, Mead & White to design and bring to life his vision of a place that contained substantial private and public areas and served as a "crossroads" of Newport life. When it opened, the Casino consisted of a three-story clubhouse. The ground floor had storefronts, and the second floor included club and reading rooms, a billiards parlor, and lodgings. The Casino also had a court tennis facility, a theater with a ballroom, numerous open-air porches, and lawn tennis courts.

Opening in the summer of 1880, the inaugural season of the Newport Casino proved to be a welcome attraction for Newport's summer residents. Its popularity grew in the late 19th and early 20th centuries. By the 1940s, though tennis still drew crowds to the site, the social club aspect of the Casino waned and the physical structure of the building suffered.

In the early 1950s, the Executive Committee of the Newport Casino discussed establishing a hall of fame and museum for tennis. The impetus for the plan came from an idea posed by then president of the Casino Jimmy Van Alen's wife, Candy. They felt that Newport—as the birthplace of championship tennis in the United States—was the ideal home for the sport's shrine.

Founded in 1954, the Hall of Fame saved the Newport Casino. Preservation efforts were recognized in 1987 when it was designated a National Historic Landmark. After 130 years, the Newport Casino is as pristine as the day it was built and will continue to inspire generations to come.

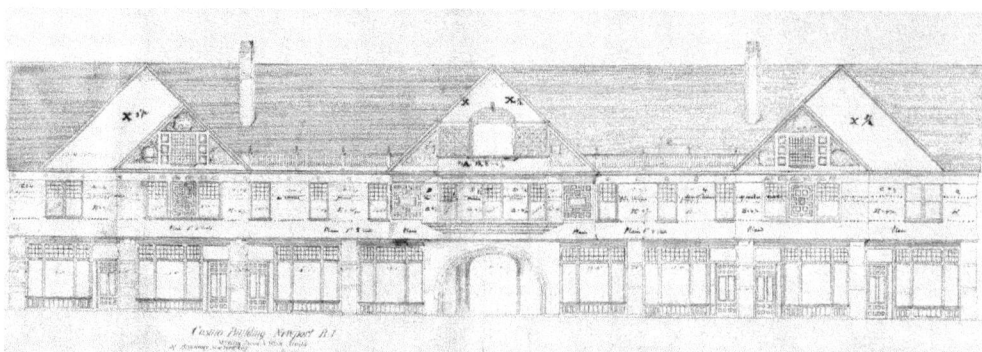

The Newport Casino was the first major building designed by McKim, Mead & White. This blueprint from late 1879 details the Bellevue Avenue elevation. Construction of the Casino complex was overseen by local contractor Nathan Barker. Breaking ground on January 8, 1880, an estimated 200 to 300 local laborers worked throughout the winter and spring to ensure the Casino would be ready for its July 1880 debut.

In late summer of 1879, James Gordon Bennett (left) bet Capt. Henry Augustus Candy to ride his polo horse up onto the Newport Reading Room's front porch. Candy took the dare further and rode straight into the club. Candy's actions were considered ungentlemanly, and his guest privileges were revoked. Enraged by his friend's treatment, Bennett decided to create a new social club. By October, he had purchased land on Bellevue Avenue.

In September 1879, a young architect named Stanford White (right) joined seasoned architects Charles Follen McKim and William Rutherford Mead. McKim was the principal mind behind the structure's construction, while White oversaw the design of the interiors (including furniture) and the Casino Theatre. Mead was the engineer, financial organizer, and "balanced mind" of the firm. (Courtesy of the Avery Library, Columbia University.)

Consisting of an intertwined "N" and "C," the logo of the Newport Casino was used on everything from official club documents and event invitations to the serving dishes used by the club members. The museum contains a number of these items in its collection, and some are presently on display.

In this c. 1885 photograph, carriages approach the entrance to the Casino. Bellevue Avenue during the Gilded Age was Newport's most prosperous and prominent address. For Newport's wealthy summer residents, a stop at the Casino was a daily occurrence. After being dropped off, visitors walked through the arcade before entering the site and seeing the lawn tennis courts.

Though the interior courtyard of the Casino has changed over its 130-year-plus history, it has always served as a breathtaking entrance that welcomes visitors to the site. This 1880 photograph highlights the fountain in the central courtyard. The one-story porch on the southern wing of the building (shown on the left side of the photograph) was expanded into the current two-story configuration in 1881.

In this c. 1900 photograph, well-heeled ladies arrive at the Newport Casino. Since its opening in 1880, both men and women were allowed to become members of the Casino. The practice of opening the membership to both sexes was a first amongst American social clubs; by 1919, women were also elected to the Board of Governors.

Newport Casino Front Court 1885

The ground floor in the northern wing of the Newport Casino (shown here in 1885) had a similar function in the 1880s as it does today, as a restaurant. The upper level contained additional club rooms for the members. Today, LaForge Casino Restaurant occupies the ground floor, and in the summer, outdoor dining allows visitors to watch tennis.

CASINO COURT AND CLOCK TOWER, NEWPORT, R. I.

Postcards highlighting details of the cultural landscape have been popular with tourists since the early 20th century. The postcard above, postmarked August 16, 1906, shows the courtyard, clock tower on the west wing, and the north wing of the Newport Casino. The clock tower is the most recognizable architectural feature on the site, and the original Tiffany clock has been maintained and functions in perfect time to this day. The c. 1905 postcard below illustrates the entrance to the curved porch that is currently known as the Horseshoe Piazza and what is now known as the Executive Porch above.

This c. 1905 postcard highlights the expansive grounds of the Newport Casino. After stepping off of the Horseshoe Piazza, visitors followed a tree-lined, curved path to the tennis courts, stadium, court tennis court, and theater at the rear of the site. Though the pathways have been altered to accommodate tennis courts and the ivy has been removed from the piazza, the view today is not much different.

Though gambling was prohibited according to the bylaws of the Club of the Newport Casino, log books within the International Tennis Hall of Fame & Museum's archives reveal that many friendly wagers took place on the tables of the billiards room, shown here as it appeared in 1885. This room now houses the Woolard Family Enshrinement Gallery.

The many tables and chairs positioned around the various club rooms were specifically designed by Stanford White for use at the Newport Casino. Several pieces of original furniture have survived to the current day and are on display in the International Tennis Hall of Fame & Museum. Today, the room houses the 1920s to 1940s galleries.

This main room of the Casino Club, known as the Reading and Conversation Room (shown here c. 1885), was located on the west side of the building on the second floor, overlooking Bellevue Avenue. The mirrored and paneled wall, shown in the background, is preserved to this day in the museum, and several pieces of the original furniture are part of the museum's permanent collection.

In this c. 1910 photograph, horse-drawn carriages begin to make way for the automobile, the new symbol of wealth and prosperity by Newport's summer colonists. At various times during the Casino's history, auto shows were hosted on the grounds, allowing members and visitors to view many of the latest models.

The original floor plan of the Newport Casino for the ground floor on the southeastern side of the building included open-air verandas. This c. 1885 photograph is taken from the southwest corner of the Horseshoe Piazza, looking northeast toward the rear of the site. Featured on the right of this photograph, a section of the porch was removed in 1905 to create a walkway to the rear of the site.

The US Navy has always been a large part of the Newport community, as shown by this World War I–era photograph. By the early 1930s, interest in the Newport Casino as a clubhouse had begun to wane. To keep the building in active use, the Board of Governors donated the second floor in 1940 to the American Red Cross and then supported the founding of an officer's club in June 1941.

When the Newport Casino first opened in 1880, there were only three tennis courts on site: the first court was for men's singles, the second was for doubles, and the third was for ladies. Women took part in the sport of tennis, both recreationally and competitively, from the sport's beginning in 1874. This c. 1920 photograph shows a crowd gathered to watch ladies play.

Keeping the grass tennis courts of the Newport Casino in prime shape required using available new technology. The lawn mower appeared in England by the mid-19th century, and the lawn roller—used to smooth and flatten—was used alongside. In this c. 1900 photograph, the Casino groundskeeper uses the roller from Philadelphia native Prof. Fairman Rogers's Newport estate on Ochre Point. (Courtesy of the Newport Historical Society.)

The layout and design of the inner courtyard, which today features a tennis court, have changed over the years. These two views show the expansive landscaping that defined the space in the 1930s and 1940s. Bands and orchestras would perform from the bandstand (gazebo), spreading their music across the grounds to entertain members and the general public alike. The central gazebo was in place until the early 1950s. By the time the National Lawn Tennis Hall of Fame opened to the public in 1954, this area had been landscaped to accommodate a tennis court.

THE NEWPORT CASINO

Tennis has always taken place on these courts, as photographs and artistic imagery from 1880 through today reveal. This photograph of the front lawn courts around 1940 was taken from the Horseshoe Piazza, looking east toward the back of the site. The far court, where the spectators are watching play, was the site of the 1881 U.S. National Championships.

In 1932, the Newport Casino hired May Sutton Bundy (class of 1956) as a tennis instructor. She won the U.S. National Women's Singles and Doubles Championships in 1904 and became the first American—male or female—to win the Wimbledon Singles Championship in 1905 and again in 1907. Her daughter Dorothy "Dodo" Bundy Cheney is also a member of the International Tennis Hall of Fame & Museum (class of 2004).

On April 18, 1953, fire ripped through the Newport Casino's north wing, causing more than $75,000 in damage. The damage, coupled with years of under-use, prompted a Providence real estate firm to offer to purchase the building. This proposal entailed tearing down this landmark to pave the way for modern development. Jimmy Van Alen (class of 1965), William McChesney Martin (class of 1982), and fellow organization leaders saved the building by establishing the National Lawn Tennis Hall of Fame.

While many recognized William McChesney Martin for his service as the Federal Reserve Board chairman from 1951 to 1970, the tennis world recognized him for his generosity in helping the game however he could. An avid player and enthusiast, Martin served as president of the National Tennis Foundation and the Hall of Fame, Inc. (1979–1985), and was instrumental in preserving the legacy of tennis and the Newport Casino.

The National Lawn Tennis Hall of Fame's dedication ceremonies took place on July 9, 1955, during a celebration of the 175th anniversary of the landing of 5,000 French soldiers to support the American Continental Army in 1780. Those standing are, from left to right, Rhode Island governor Dennis Roberts (1951–1959), Count Rochambeau, Rhode Island senator Theodore F. Green, Newport Casino vice president James Van Alen, and Tennis Hall of Fame president William Clothier.

On July 9, 1955, Grace Kelly, later Princess Consort of Monaco, and Peruvian ambassador Fernando Berckemeyer (right) joined Henry Heffernan (left), chairman of the Executive Committee of the Newport Casino, in the dedication celebrations of the National Lawn Tennis Hall of Fame. It also marked the first class of Hall of Famers inducted.

The picturesque beauty that the Newport Casino was known for from the moment the doors were opened in 1880 still shines today, as evidenced by this summer 2009 photograph. The Horseshoe Court hosts exhibition matches, while the second floor of the Casino serves as the museum. Throughout the year, visitors from around the world make a stop at the Newport Casino. Many options await visitors, such as going to the museum, enjoying an audio tour of the galleries, walking the manicured grounds, playing on the grass courts, shopping in the retail stores, and dining at LaForge Casino Restaurant. (Photograph by Cailin Mateleska.)

2

The U.S. National

Championships

In 1881, the United States National Lawn Tennis Association (USNLTA) desired a location to host the first U.S. National Championships. The Newport Casino was selected, and the birth of American tournament tennis began. The Newport Casino hosted the U.S. National Championships from 1881 through 1914. Beginning in 1915, the U.S. Nationals moved to the West Side Tennis Club in Forest Hills, New York. In 1978, Flushing Meadows became the new site. Today, that championship is known as the US Open.

The first U.S. Nationals began on August 31, 1881, with 25 contestants. Play ensued on the grass courts accompanied by a string quartet playing classical music. Dick Sears, a Bostonian, emerged as the country's first champion. In its 34 years at the Newport Casino, the U.S. Nationals witnessed the emergence of many early tennis champions. Dick Sears won the first seven championships before retiring undefeated. He was succeeded by Henry Slocum, Oliver Campbell, Robert Wrenn, and Malcolm Whitman, who each won the singles championship multiple times. The first decade of the 20th century saw the brilliance of William Larned, who equaled Dick Sears's seven singles championships.

On the doubles side, Sears teamed with James Dwight to form the first great American doubles team. They captured five championships before ceding to other great doubles champions. In 1899, Dwight Davis won the first of three doubles championships with Holcombe Ward. During this time, Davis established the International Lawn Tennis Challenge Trophy, affectionately known as the Davis Cup, the annual international men's team competition. At the U.S. Nationals, Holcombe Ward paired with Beals C. Wright to capture three titles before Fred Alexander and Harold Hackett won four consecutive doubles titles.

By the early 1900s, tennis' popularity continued to grow. Though still an attractive summer retreat, many within the USNLTA felt that Newport was too isolated and not substantial enough to accommodate the increasing number of tournament spectators. The desire for a more centralized location was vocalized, and following the 1914 Championships, the tournament moved to New York.

The first U.S. National Singles Championship was contested at the Newport Casino in 1881. Conducted under the auspices of the United States National Lawn Tennis Association (USNLTA), the first championship consisted of 25 participants. Players competed on the grass courts accompanied by a string quartet playing classical music. Dick Sears (class of 1955) won the championship without losing a set by besting William Glyn in the final 6-0, 6-3, 6-2.

Dick Sears, a Boston native, was the first dominant American tennis player. He captured the U.S. Nationals seven consecutive years (1881–1887), losing only three sets in the championship round before retiring undefeated. Sears became president of the USNLTA and was inducted into the International Tennis Hall of Fame & Museum's first class in 1955.

James Dwight (left) and Dick Sears (right) were arguably the first great American doubles team. From 1882 to 1887, they captured five U.S. National Doubles Championships. Regarded as the "Father of American Tennis," Dwight (class of 1956) was instrumental in the formation of the USNLTA, the first U.S. National Championships, and the first Davis Cup series in 1900.

This print, based on a photograph by Historic Alman Photographers, appeared in the September 5, 1885, issue of *Harper's Weekly* under the title "Lawn Tennis at Newport—The Tournament from the Upper Balcony at the Casino." The image shows tennis being played on the front lawn courts below. The court closest to the balcony was the site of the first U.S. Nationals in 1881.

Attending a tennis match at the U.S. Nationals was often considered a prominent affair. Men and women dressed in their best clothes, and it was reported that the female summer colonists never wore the same dress twice. The grandstand was usually sold out, many spectators having purchased their tickets in advance.

One year after losing to Dick Sears in his final U.S. National Championships, Henry Slocum Jr. finally became champion. In 1888 and 1889, Slocum was ranked No. 1 in the country, having captured two consecutive singles championships and one doubles title (1899). He later served as president of the USNLTA and was inducted into the International Tennis Hall of Fame & Museum's first class in 1955.

Tennis fashion for men at the Newport Casino in the 1880s consisted of coat and tie, flannel shirts and pants, and shoes or boots. Tom Pettitt (class of 1982), seated third from the right, was the Newport Casino's first tennis professional. Pettitt taught both lawn tennis and court tennis, although he gained greater fame in court tennis. He won the World Court Tennis Singles Championship in 1885.

Hundreds of tennis enthusiasts gathered around the front lawn courts to witness a semifinal match between Oliver Campbell (class of 1955) and Bob Huntington in 1890. In a classic five-set match, Campbell came back from two sets to one down to win 3-6, 6-2, 5-7, 6-2, 6-1. Campbell then prevailed in the Challenge Round over defending champion Henry Slocum (class of 1955) to win the first of three consecutive singles championships.

Played on the grass court adjacent to the court tennis facility, this 1891 match featured Fred Hovey (class of 1974), who twice won the US Intercollegiate Singles at Harvard University. Hovey enjoyed great success as a player and was ranked in the top 10 from 1890 to 1896, which included being No. 1 in 1895. Hovey reached four singles championships (winning in 1895) and three doubles (winning in 1893 and 1894).

On August 26, 1891, before a large crowd and the Ocean House Hotel (now demolished) in the background, Oliver Campbell faced off against Clarence Hobart for the championship. Hobart was making his first appearance in the finals, while Campbell sought to defend his title. In a tough five-set match, Campbell prevailed 2-6, 7-5, 7-9, 6-1, 6-2 and won the second of three consecutive titles.

Ball boys for the 1892 U.S. National Championships pose for a group photograph on the stairs of the East Porch, located by the court tennis facility. Dressed in shirts, ties, short pants, and caps, the ball boys were local residents who assisted with the U.S. Nationals and other tennis events at the Newport Casino.

During the second decade of the U.S. National Championships, the most dominant player was Robert Wrenn (class of 1955). A Chicago native and graduate of Harvard University, Wrenn appeared in five consecutive finals, winning four times (1893, 1894, 1896, and 1897). He won once in doubles (1895). Wrenn was the first left-hander to win the championship. He later served with Theodore Roosevelt in the Spanish-American War.

Dwight Filley Davis (class of 1956) was a great doubles player and captured three U.S. National Doubles Championships (1899–1901) with Holcombe Ward (class of 1956). However, he is best known for creating the Davis Cup, the annual international team competition that bears his name. He later served as Pres. Calvin Coolidge's secretary of war from 1925 to 1929.

Regarded as the best doubles team at the dawn of the 20th century, England's Reginald and Laurence Doherty (class of 1980) became the first foreign-born champions of the U.S. National Doubles Championships. The Dohertys won twice in 1902 and 1903, both times in straight sets. They later made their mark in Davis Cup play with a perfect 5-0 record as a team.

William Larned (class of 1956) dominated the U.S. National Championships in the first decade of the 20th century. From 1901 to 1911, Larned appeared in eight finals, winning seven times, and tying Dick Sears for most U.S. National Singles Championships. Larned was a consistent player, and in 19 years from 1891 to 1911, he missed the semifinals only twice while compiling a 61-12 record.

Beals C. Wright (class of 1956) was a consistent player during the first decade of the 20th century and appeared in four singles championships. His lone title came in 1905 when he defeated Holcombe Ward 6-1, 6-2, 11-9. En route to the finals, Wright defeated William Clothier (class of 1956), a future champion, and William Larned, who defeated him in 1901.

In the 1912 U.S. Nationals quarterfinals, Maurice McLoughlin (class of 1957) faced off against Richard Norris Williams II (class of 1957), who had survived the sinking of the RMS *Titanic* months earlier. A native of Nevada, McLoughlin was a perennial contender from 1911 to 1914, the last four years the U.S. National Championships were held in Newport. He won the singles twice (1912 and 1913) and the doubles three times (1912–1914).

3

NEWPORT SOCIETY

Newport—the City by the Sea—was the "Queen of Resorts" during the Gilded Age. The late 19th and early 20th centuries were an era of extravagant displays of wealth and excess within America's aristocracy. Newport, with its proximity to urban areas such as Boston, New York, and Philadelphia, captured the imaginations of countless numbers of people as the ultimate refuge from the hustle and bustle of life in the metropolitan scene and became the summer playground for the upper echelons of society.

As soon as the Newport Casino opened its doors in 1880, the wealthy summer residents—families with last names such as Vanderbilt, Astor, or Oelrichs—and members of the city's year-round population came out to play. The Newport Casino was the first public-private establishment in the country and offered numerous amusements, many of which have continued to the present day. Such social activities included lawn tennis, concerts, court tennis, croquet, horse shows, flower shows, art installations, dancing, auto shows, dining, lawn bowling, and theatrical performances. The Newport Casino published programs each season that not only included the schedule of events for the complex but also society gossip from around the country and abroad in columns titled "Heard at the Casino."

During the 1920s and 1930s, the social aspects of this resort town appealed to tennis players as much as the thrill of competing in the Newport Casino Invitational Tournament. This was the golden age of tennis, and the athletes were bona fide celebrities, and as such, partook in the summer parties. Players described Newport at this time as the greatest party/tennis tournament of the circuit.

Newport continues to attract visitors from around the globe. Today, the International Tennis Hall of Fame & Museum and the Newport Casino is open to the public year-round and offers a multitude of activities for all facets of modern society.

Though the grounds were open to the public, the Casino Club was still exclusive in the Gilded Age. One had to be a shareholder, annual member, paying subscriber, or introduced by the Executive Committee of the Newport Casino to access the amenities. The Board of Governors, shown here around 1890, voted on new members using a white or black billiard ball; two black balls denied one membership. (Courtesy of the Newport Historical Society.)

The confluence of America's aristocracy at the Newport Casino proved to be an inviting spot for media to eavesdrop on tantalizing gossip. In 1909, this intrusion caused the Casino's governors to bar public entrance to the grounds except for tennis tournaments, horse shows, and Sunday evening concerts. Newspapers fought the ban by reporting, "only the graveyard is more exclusive." The governors quickly admitted defeat, and freedom of access was restored.

Members of the Casino from around 1890 are, from left to right, (first row, seated on ground) Edgerton Winthrop and two unidentified men; (second row) Hollis Hunnewell, Rose Post, Thomas Howard, Lizzie LaMontagne, Charlotte Winthrop, Brocky Cutting, Annie Cutting, an unidentified man, Georgie Berryman, and Charles Carroll; (third row) Belle Wilson, Pearl Carley, Stanley Mortimer, Eleanor Winslow, Mrs. I.T. Burden, Kitty LaMontagne, Julian Potter, Woodbury Kane, Mrs. Prescott Lawrence, and an unidentified man.

This extravagant weekly publication began in 1886 and went bankrupt in 1932. The summer colonists purchased the *Bulletin* to learn about the Casino's schedule of events, names of the governors and stockholders, and the current local and international gossip. The publication also featured advertisements, photographs of various Newport homes, and information about other local entertainment.

A SUNDAY NIGHT CONCERT AT THE CASINO

Music was a central component to the entertainment at the Newport Casino. Concerts, including performances by the Boston Symphony Orchestra, the New York Philharmonic, and the Philadelphia and Cleveland Symphonies, were a daily occurrence during the high season from 1880 through the 1940s. This print, titled "A Sunday Night Concert at the Casino," by Henry Pott, appeared in the July 1901 issue of *Harper's Monthly*.

In this undated photograph, summer residents pose with canine companions. Leashed dogs were allowed on-site and often accompanied their owners for socializing. In the 1890s, Mrs. Stuyvesant Fish, known as "Mamie," and her social advisor and fellow prankster Harry Lehr "dognapped" a fellow socialite's dachshund, covered it with flour, and released it at the Casino amongst a crowd of society members dressed in their finest attire.

The 1892 summer colonists are, from left to right, (first row, seated on ground) Count Sierstorpf, Victor Sorehan, Duncan Elliot, and Winthrop Rutherford; (second row) Mrs. George Barclay, J.F.D. Lanier, Edith Cushing, Mrs. L.M. Rutherford, Mrs. John Astor, and Mrs. Whitney Warren; (third row) Mrs. J. Borden Harriman, Belgian minister M. LeGhait, Mrs. Ogden Mills, Miss Tooker, Mrs. Victor Sorehan, Mrs. Sidney Dillon Ripley, Mrs. W. Butler Duncan, Count Boni de Castellane, Mrs. W.R. Travers, and Frederick Beach; (fourth row) Thomas Cushing, Mrs. Fernando Yznaga, Señor Padelia of the Spanish Legation, Anna Sands, Mrs. Stuyvesant Fish, Whitney Warren, Fernando Yznaga, Maud Livingston, Lloyd Warren, Sallie Hargous, and Hamilton W. Cary.

Many of the summer residents were equine enthusiasts, and it was fitting that the Newport Casino's expansive grounds were used for horse shows following completion of the tennis tournaments, as shown in this 1905 postcard. From September 5 to 7, 1898, the first Newport Horse Show took place. Horse aficionados Reginald Vanderbilt and Oliver Belmont were two of the moving forces behind the development of the annual Newport Horse Show.

In this c. 1915 photograph, Newport Horse Show officials, participants, and a young groomsman (seated on the ground) gather at the center of the show ring. In the background, one can see the cupola that graces the northeast corner of the Newport Casino's main building. "Judge" William H. Moore is standing third from the left, and Reginald Vanderbilt is standing fifth from the right.

Society's members would arrive at their boxes smartly dressed to witness some of the finest horses, carriages, and riders the country had to offer. One of the regular competitors in the early 20th century was "Judge" William Henry Moore (1848–1922), a prominent and wealthy financier and attorney. In 1908, the *New York Times* reported that Moore submitted 58 entries into that year's horse show.

Reginald Claypoole Vanderbilt, often considered the black sheep of America's wealthiest family, was an avid horseman who owned a 280-acre estate, named Sandy Point Farm, in nearby Portsmouth. He is shown here competing at the Newport Horse Show in 1915, exhibiting in the class for large pairs. Reginald, the fourth son and heir of Cornelius Vanderbilt II, was also the father of Gloria Vanderbilt and grandfather of Anderson Cooper.

The Newport Horse Show was extremely popular with the summer colonists of Newport who purchased the detailed yearly programs. This annual event, signaling the close of the summer season, first took place in 1898 and continued at the Newport Casino (except during World War I) through 1928. Today, a horse-shaped weather vane on Bill Talbert Center Court pays homage to this event and marks the location where stables once stood.

1924

OFFICIAL

CATALOGUE

Newport Horse Show

Member Association of American Horse Shows, Inc.

NEWPORT CASINO

August 28th, 29th, 30th

In this undated photograph, a well-dressed woman poses with her child in front of a crowd sitting in the stands at the Newport Casino. Unfortunately, it is not known what event this photograph documents, but it is amusing to note that the child the woman is holding appears to be sitting in a trophy.

Mrs. Hermann Oelrichs, known as "Tessie," was one of the grand dames of American aristocratic society. She met her future husband, Hermann, while attending tennis matches at the Newport Casino in 1889 and is shown here with Ambassador James W. Gerard around 1915. Rosecliff, the Oelrichs' summer home in Newport, was designed and built by Stanford White and is now owned and operated by the Preservation Society of Newport County.

William Vincent Astor (1891–1959), son of John Jacob Astor IV and grandson of "The Mrs. Astor," Caroline Astor, spent summer holidays at his family's Newport home, named Beechwood. The home was built by Andrew Jackson Dowling and Calvert Vaux. William is shown playing tennis at the Newport Casino around 1910.

Seated amongst friends in 1908 holding a tennis racquet, Eleonora Sears (class of 1968) was a talented athlete who excelled in many sports, including equestrianism, golf, walking, and tennis. She hailed from an accomplished Boston tennis family. Her father, Fred Sears, was one of the first to play tennis in the United States, and her uncle, Dick Sears, was the inaugural U.S. Nationals Champion.

GARDEN CLUB OF AMERICA
JUNE 28 1923
NEWPORT CASINO.

With so many of the estates in Newport boasting luscious landscapes, their owners were proud members of the Garden Club and competed in annual flower shows organized by the Garden Club and the Newport Horticultural Society. These were popular attractions held at the Casino,

as evidenced by this large gathering of the Garden Club of America members here in 1923. For many years, a flower show was held at the Newport Casino. Today, the Preservation Society of Newport County hosts an annual Newport Flower Show on a weekend in June.

Finely dressed spectators crowd around the tennis court and stand on chairs in order to watch William Larned take on Bill Clothier at the 1909 U.S. National Championships. Clothier pushed the match to five sets, but ultimately Larned prevailed 6-1, 6-2, 5-7, 1-6, 6-1. This marked Clothier's final time as a contender for the championship. Larned would go on to win twice more.

Music was always a central part of the Casino entertainment offerings, and the introduction of a gazebo in the courtyard in the 1930s (not shown here) allowed music to be heard across the whole site. It was reported that, at times, the grounds were hardly large enough to accommodate the throngs of people coming to listen to the performances.

4

Newport Casino Invitational Tournament

Writing in the September 1, 1915, issue of *American Lawn Tennis*, publisher and editor Stephen Wallis Merrihew noted, "Newport's first annual invitation tournament was an unqualified success. A fair description of it would deal only in superlatives."

Merrihew's favorable description of the Newport Casino Invitational Tournament was both fair and accurate. Initially, there may have been some concerns regarding what would happen to the venue with the U.S. National Championships moving to Forest Hills following the conclusion of the 1914 event. It quickly became clear, however, that from the time the first ball was struck, the Casino Invitational would prove more than an ample substitute for the U.S. National Championships that had been held at the Newport Casino for the past 34 years. Many spectators commented that they even preferred the Casino Invitational's smaller draw size, which made for more exciting tennis throughout the course of the entire competition.

The appeal and success of the Casino Invitational is evident in the fact that it remains the longest-running tournament to have been contested at the Newport Casino. It was held on no less than 48 occasions between 1915 and 1967, with the tournament only being cancelled in 1917–1918 and 1943–1945 for both of the world wars. It was a truly global competition that saw players from the United States, Great Britain, Spain, Australia, Japan, and many other countries.

Many of the most notable legends in the sport of tennis came from all over the world to play in the Casino Invitational. From Hall of Famers Bill Tilden, Don Budge, and Fred Perry to Frank Sedgman, Tony Trabert, Ken Rosewall, and Rod Laver, many of the greats graced the lawns of the Newport Casino every summer as part of their match preparation for the U.S. Nationals. The Casino Invitational was a unique and popular tournament with players and fans alike, and it will always have a special place in the history of tennis in the "City by the Sea."

The year 1915 marked the first year that the Casino Invitational was contested following the departure of the U.S. National Championships from the Newport Casino to Forest Hills, New York. Many in the audience reported that the Casino Invitational proved more entertaining than the U.S. Nationals, as the Casino Invitational's smaller draw size meant that the match-ups were

intriguing from beginning to end. Dressed in their finest suits and dresses, spectators poured in from all over the region for a fascinating week of tennis that culminated with an enthralling final that saw 1914 U.S. Nationals Singles champion Richard Norris Williams II win the inaugural event over countryman Maurice McLoughlin 5-7, 6-4, 6-3, 6-3.

In 1916, just the second year of the Casino Invitational, Ichiya Kumagai became the first foreign player to win the title. Kumagai fought his way to the championship by defeating the more celebrated Bill Johnston (class of 1958) by a score of 6-1, 9-7, 5-7, 2-6, 9-7.

The Newport Casino ball boys in 1918 included No. 45 Skelly Fagan, No. 5 George Boyle, No. 14 Edward "Mucka" Curran, No. 6 Ed "Flat Nose" Adamson, No. 44 Jack Murphy, No. 35 Woody Ring, No. 19 John Reilly, No. 30 Tom Finn, No. 26 Art Freshman, No. 16 Skeet Lynch (behind No. 41), No. 46 Walter Pike (behind No. 43), No. 33 Lenny DeSantis, No. 41 Midge "Stew" Glen, No. 43 Tony DeSantis, as well as Harry Beach, Jake Aronson, Jim Tracy, Jim Martin, and George Ring.

The bespectacled Watson Washburn (class of 1965) prepares to lunge for a forehand in competition play. Washburn defeated former U.S. Nationals and Casino Invitational champion Richard Norris Williams II to win the 1921 Casino Invitational singles title. He defeated his compatriot in five entertaining sets 4-6, 6-3, 1-6, 6-2, 6-2.

Pictured here are American tennis icons Bill Tilden (class of 1959) and Bill Johnston. Known as "Big Bill" and "Little Bill," they formed one of the greatest rivalries in the sport. They squared off against each other in the 1919 Casino Invitational final, and as so frequently happened over the course of their rivalry, "Big Bill" got the better of "Little Bill" 8-6, 7-5, 6-1.

George Lott (class of 1964) receives the singles trophy from James Cushman after he defeated compatriot John Van Ryn (class of 1963) in five lopsided sets 2-6, 6-0, 3-6, 6-2, 6-0 to take the 1928 championship. Lott also teamed with John Doeg (class of 1962) to win the doubles title over Wilmer Allison (class of 1963) and Van Ryn.

Rufus Davis held the post of head of umpires in the 1920s and 1930s at the Newport Casino. Davis was excellent at his job and, as a result, he was very popular with spectators and players alike. He was particularly known for his "pleasant voice," which only added to his popularity whether he was giving directions or officiating a match.

Bill Tilden joined forces with American Frank Hunter (class of 1961) to defeat the tough combination of Wilbur Coen Jr. and Harris Coggeshell in the 1930 doubles final. In the near court, Tilden and Hunter squeaked out a five-set victory 6-3, 6-4, 0-6, 3-6, 6-2. The win marked Bill Tilden's last trip to the winner's circle in Newport as he turned professional later that year.

Ellsworth Vines (class of 1962) proved an invincible force at the Newport Casino. He defeated England's Fred Perry (class of 1975) 6-2, 6-4, 6-8, 6-2 in 1931 before going on to defeat Wilmer Allison 6-4, 6-3, 6-3 the following year to defend his title. In doubles, he partnered with Keith Gledhill to take three consecutive doubles titles from 1931 to 1933.

Though not as well known as his granddaughter Brooke Shields, Frank Shields (class of 1964) was quite the tennis star in his day. Surrounded by smiling ball boys, Shields receives the singles trophy from head professional Tom Pettitt in 1933 where he won the title 1-6, 11-9, 6-1, 6-3 over Wilmer Allison. (Courtesy of Wide World Photo.)

One of the most stable Davis Cup doubles teams for the United States was John Van Ryn and Wilmer Allison. Van Ryn talks to James Cushman during a trophy presentation, while his partner Allison is standing by. Van Ryn and Allison won the Casino Invitational doubles title in 1934 over George Lott and Lester Stoefen 3-6, 6-1, 14-12, 3-6, 6-3. (Courtesy of Rotofoto, Inc.)

Newport Casino
Umbrella **TT** Seat **1**
INVITATION TENNIS TOURNAMENT
Umbrella | Est'b Price $68.18 / Tax Paid 6.82 } Total $75.00

Newport Casino
NEWPORT, R. I.
This Ticket Admits to the Grounds and
Umbrella **TT** Seat **1**
Invitation Tennis Tournament
AUGUST 12, 1935
Umbrella | Est'b Price $68.18 / Tax Paid 6.82 } Total $75.00

This is a ticket to the 1935 Casino Invitational. The ticket entitled the holder to one of the coveted umbrella seats, as well as viewing some spectacular tennis competition that included the great Don Budge (class of 1964), who made history in 1938 by becoming the first man to win all four majors in a single year to claim the first Grand Slam in tennis.

Before television sets were common place, radio broadcasting was the chosen media for informing the public about the news of the day. Depicted here, broadcasters from the National Broadcasting Corporation (NBC) can be seen broadcasting the play-by-play of the 1938 Casino Invitational, which was dominated by Don Budge who won the title over Sidney Wood (class of 1964) in three short sets 6-3, 6-3, 6-2.

Don Budge is seen here with his good friend and doubles partner Gene Mako (class of 1973) at Forest Hills in 1938 after Budge defeated Mako to win the Grand Slam. Budge not only won the Casino Invitational singles title in 1935 but also in 1937 and 1938. In addition, he teamed with Mako to win the doubles championship from 1936 to 1938. (Courtesy of Max Peter Haas.)

Known for the professional tour he founded, Jack Kramer (class of 1968) was a phenomenal player. He teamed with Ted Schroeder (class of 1966) to win the Casino Invitational doubles title in 1941 over Frank Parker (class of 1966) and Don McNeill (class of 1965) 4-6, 6-4, 8-6, 6-1 and in 1946 over Bill Talbert (class of 1967) and Bob Falkenburg (class of 1974) 7-5, 8-10, 9-7, 6-3. (Courtesy of *World Tennis*.)

The stands were packed in 1949 when the always-colorful Richard "Pancho" Gonzales (class of 1968) faced off against fellow American Gardnar Mulloy (class of 1972) in the men's singles final. Gonzales wielded one of the greatest serves in the history of the game, and it aided him in earning the win over Mulloy in an enthralling four-set final 10-8, 9-11, 6-3, 6-4. (Courtesy of Lloyd Pauley.)

The year 1950 was a good year for Ted Schroeder, who won the Casino Invitational men's singles title over Art "Tappy" Larsen (class of 1969) in three sets 6-3, 7-5, 6-4. Schroeder is seen receiving the trophy from Eleonora Sears. Schroeder reached the doubles final with partner Budge Patty (class of 1977) before Patty was injured and forced to default the final match. (Courtesy of Lloyd Pauley.)

Seen here at Forest Hills in 1951, Frank Sedgman (class of 1979) and Ken McGregor (class of 1999) were the first to achieve a calendar year Grand Slam in doubles. They brought their brand of doubles to Newport and earned a hard-fought finals victory—5-7, 9-7, 3-6, 9-7, 6-3—over Vic Seixas (class of 1971) and Bill Talbert in 1952. (Courtesy of *American Lawn Tennis*.)

Tony Trabert (class of 1970) had a remarkable career, but his banner year was 1953. The American won three of the four majors that year, and his dominance extended to the Casino Invitational. He fought back from a two-set deficit to defeat Vic Seixas 5-7, 0-6, 6-4, 8-6, 6-3, before teaming with Seixas to win the doubles over Ham Richardson and Bill Talbert 6-4, 6-3, 6-3.

Those pictured at the conclusion of the 1955 men's doubles final are, from left to right, Kosei Kamo, Vic Seixas, Candace Van Alen, Ham Richardson, and Atsushi Miyagi. Richardson and Seixas defeated the Japanese pair 3-6, 6-1, 6-4. Candy Van Alen, wife of International Tennis Hall of Fame & Museum founder Jimmy Van Alen, presented the trophy. (Courtesy of Lloyd Pauley.)

Lunging for the ball at the 1968 US Open in Forest Hills, Australian Ken "Muscles" Rosewall (class of 1980) competed in the 1956 Casino Invitational and was rewarded for his efforts by handily beating Ham Richardson 6-0, 8-6, 6-2 in the singles final. Rosewall teamed with Neale Fraser (class of 1984) to take the doubles title in straight sets over Mike Green and Mike Franks 6-2, 9-7, 6-3.

Preparing to hit a serve at the 1969 Wimbledon Championships, Rod "Rocket" Laver (class of 1981) is the only player to have achieved the Grand Slam twice. Prior to hitting his stride, Laver graced the lawns of the Newport Casino by competing in the 1960 Casino Invitational. He took the title over home-crowd favorite Butch Buchholz (class of 2005) that year with a 6-1, 6-8, 6-1, 6-2 victory.

It was a couple of Australians who contested the final in Newport in 1967, the year of the last Casino Invitational. Finalist Owen Davidson (class of 2010) is seen here with Jimmy Van Alen, who is presenting the cup to winner Bill Bowrey. Davidson and Bowrey also won the doubles crown in straight sets over Ray Ruffels and Brian Tobin (class of 2003) 6-3, 6-4.

5

CASINO THEATRE

AND COURT TENNIS

Along with the inspiring architecture of the main building and the historic grass courts and landscaped grounds, the Newport Casino complex includes two other remarkable structures both completed in 1880.

The elaborate Casino Theatre was designed by Stanford White to be a centerpiece of Newport artistic and social performances. It was also the scene of dances, musical recitals, poetry readings, vaudeville acts, concerts, magic shows, lectures, and theatrical performances. The restored theater space features gold-trimmed and stenciled walls, graceful arched galleries, and a sky-blue, vaulted ceiling from which is suspended a magnificent chandelier.

In its early years, this Newport jewel hosted celebrated appearances by notables, such as Oscar Wilde and Julia Ward Howe. The theater operated off and on throughout the 20th century, its stage graced by a succession of big-name stars, such as Basil Rathbone, Olivia de Havilland, Vincent Price, Tallulah Bankhead, Will Rogers, Orson Welles, Helen Hayes, and Lillian Gish.

Due to structural concerns, the theater closed its doors in the 1980s and sat unused for nearly 30 years until its grand reopening in 2010, following a $5.2-million restoration.

Next to the Casino Theatre, and overlooking the original grass courts of the 1881 U.S. National Championships, is one of only nine court tennis courts in the country. The court facility, home to the National Tennis Club, is the second built in the United States and is the only one open to play by the general public.

Court tennis (also known as real tennis or royal tennis) dates back to the Renaissance and is very different in play to lawn tennis. High walls with sloping roofs and various openings enclose the Newport Casino's cavernous 90-by-40-foot court, which is marked with lines across its width to measure a part of the game called the "chase." Complexities in the rules of the game allow much more finesse in strategy and tactic than in modern lawn tennis, while still requiring athletic prowess.

The court tennis court at the National Tennis Club is in regular use throughout the year, hosting high-level national and international championship competitions, as well as lessons for beginners and professionals alike.

From the day of its opening, the Casino Theatre was meant to serve as a luxurious showcase for Newport society. Elegantly dressed Newport society members arrived in coaches to attend the numerous evening dances held in the Casino Theatre throughout the summer. For a small price, local townspeople could watch the festivities from the galleries above.

The Casino Theatre served the community not only as a venue for entertainment, such as dances, plays, and music, but also as a place for public lectures from the likes of Oscar Wilde. Wilde's stop at the Casino Theatre in 1882 was greeted with enthusiasm, despite his description of Newport in a letter that year as a place "where idleness ranks among the virtues."

PHONE · Newport 400-401

NEWPORT·R·I

CASINO THEATRE

The Casino Theatre was used for a variety of cultural, entertainment, and educational events from musical concerts to lectures, literary readings, and even social luncheons and teas. While primarily a venue for the Newport social elite, the Casino Theatre was also a gathering place for working families, who could attend the events or observe from the galleries for a reduced admission price. Major orchestra symphonies traveled from Boston, New York, and Philadelphia to give performances up through the first half of the 20th century. As the *New York Times* noted in 1886, "The poor mechanic and clerk can take his wife and children to the Casino every Sunday night and listen to a capital concert for 25¢ per head."

NEWPORT CASINO

Program of Music

by the

NEWPORT
SYMPHONY
ORCHESTRA

Director, THEOPHIL WENDT
F.R.A.M. (London)

for the
WEEK BEGINNING
JUNE 30TH
1930

The Baldwin Piano is the Official Piano of the Newport Casino Orchestra

Program
Newport Casino Theatre
NEWPORT, R. I.

presents

BASIL RATHBONE

In

"The Gioconda Smile"

WEEK OF JULY 9 — JULY 14

1951

The original theater auditorium seating was removable, allowing the space to serve as a community ballroom in addition to the stage performances held there. A 1920s renovation included the addition of fixed seating in the auditorium, which precluded the dances of early years and shifted the focus of the theater from social gatherings to public performances. The heydays of the Casino Theatre stage performances extended through the 1950s under a series of theater managers and companies. As shown in these programs, stars like Basil Rathbone and Gloria Swanson made regular stops to perform in Newport.

Program
Newport Casino Theatre
Newport, R. I.

— presents —

GLORIA SWANSON

— in —

"RED LETTER DAY"

by

ANDREW ROSENTHAL

with

BUDDY ROGERS

AUGUST 17 — AUGUST 22

1959

The restoration work of the Casino Theatre, which was in the planning stages for four years, took just over a year to complete. The project, which cost $5.2 million, was funded primarily through donations and grants, including a Save America's Treasures grant from the National Park Service. The project was overseen by architect Martha Werenfels and construction manager Jim Farrar. The elaborate restoration was recognized with a 2010 Rhody Award for the project's contribution to the preservation of Rhode Island's historic resources.

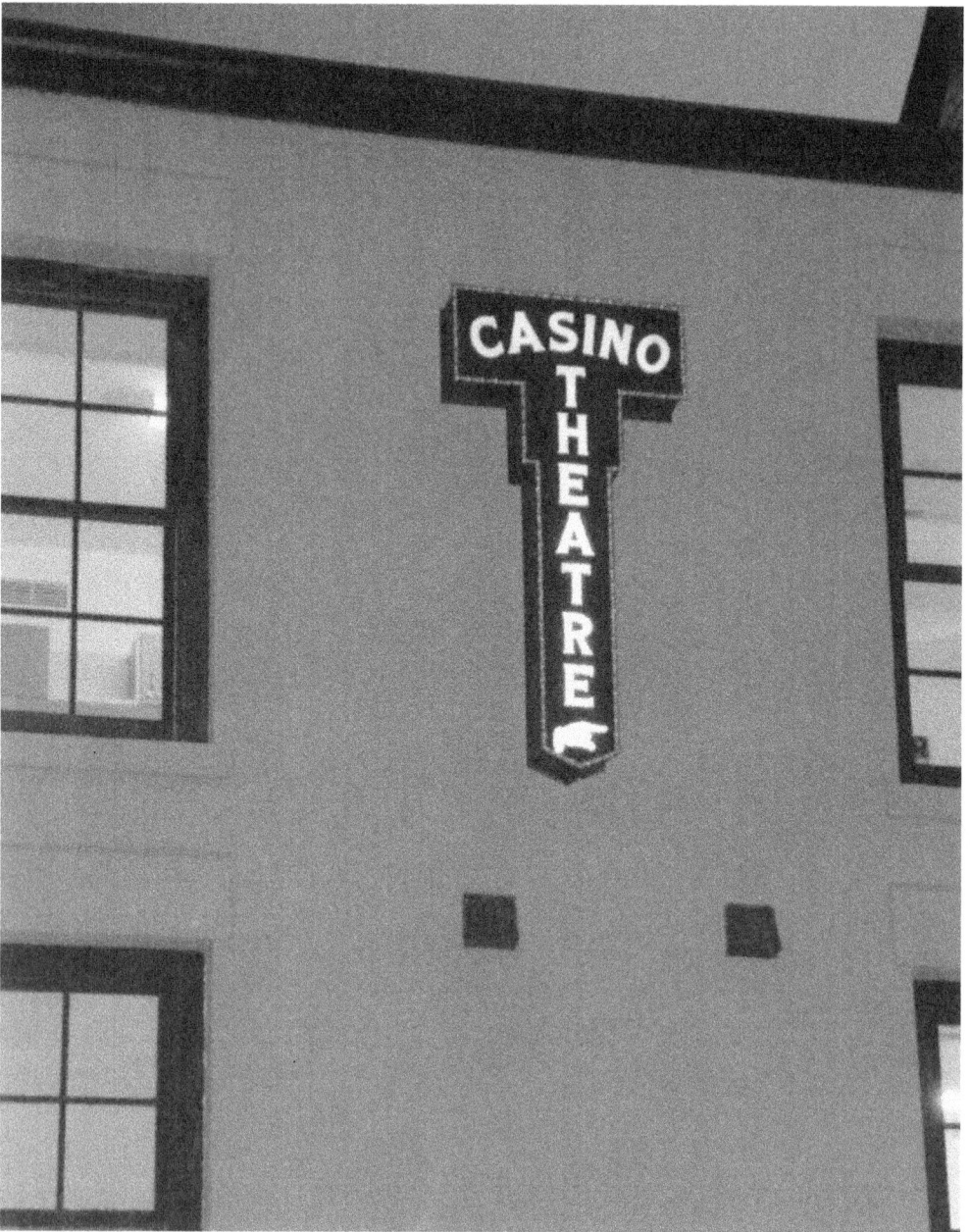

The Casino Theatre is the first and only remaining Stanford White theater in existence. It functioned as a community gathering place for both the summer residents of Newport, as well as the families who lived here year-round. The entrance to the theater, with this restored lighted sign, is situated on Freebody Street, directly across from Freebody Park, home for many years to the famous Newport Jazz and Folk Festivals. Salve Regina University, also located in Newport, manages and maintains the theater as an educational facility for its Department of Performing Arts during the academic year, making the building available to other groups for theatrical productions, films, concerts, lectures, and public events.

Attention to detail in the elaborate 2010 restoration allows theater patrons a glimpse into Newport's Gilded Age. Details such as gold stenciling on the walls; plaster medallions and raised motifs; thick, red carpeting; and finely detailed decorations on the walls, trim, and balconies recall the former glory of the space. The same Michigan-based seating company that made the original seats restored them. The seats have been color-matched to the originals and even include antiquated gentlemen's top hat holders underneath. While the main auditorium maintains the illusion of stepping back in time, including a functional orchestra pit, the basement and backstage have been converted to modern classrooms, dressing rooms, storage areas, workshops, and office space to accommodate the demands of a functioning theater department.

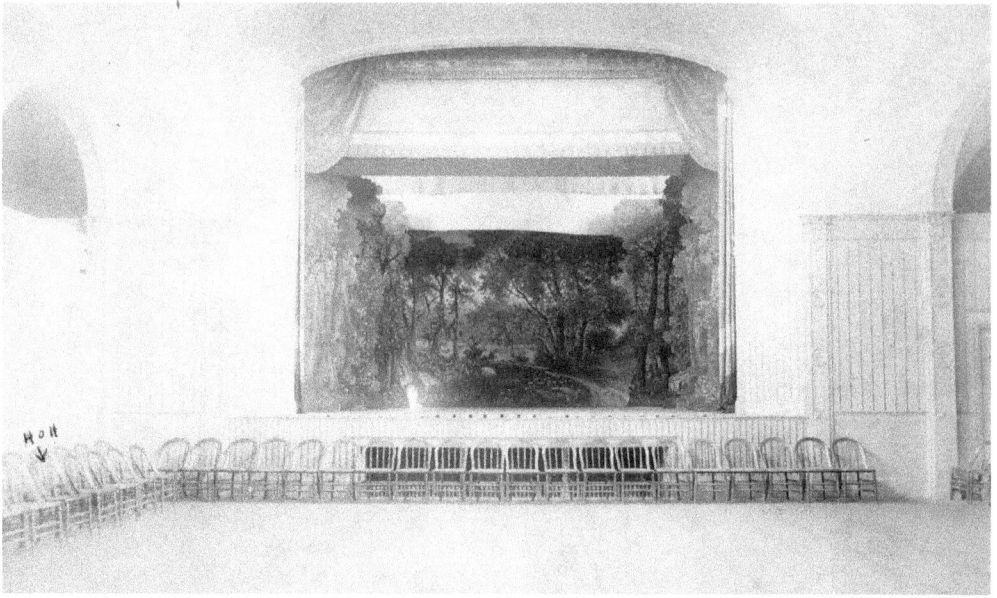

Unused since the early 1980s, the Casino Theatre presented many challenges to the craftsmen and artisans who restored its former glory in just over a year of dedicated work. Work began in the summer of 2009, and the theater was reopened in October 2010. Original fixtures and decorative embellishments were kept wherever possible, while adding modern conveniences and necessities, such as a raised floor for better viewing from the back seats and modern lighting and audio-visual equipment for greater flexibility in performances. The photograph above shows the auditorium in 1885 when it had its removable chairs pushed aside for a dance; the restored theater features fixed seating. (Below, courtesy of Kim Fuller Photography.)

The extensive project at the Casino Theatre included replacing the facility's signature Shingle-style exterior, installing a full fire suppression system and a new heating and cooling system, improving the electrical system, and raising a new 1880s-inspired chandelier. In addition, new bathrooms were installed, the dressing rooms were completely overhauled, and a green room and costume shop were developed in the area beneath the stage. The building is also accessible to those with disabilities. The theater's historic value and stunning detail were taken into account in every phase of the project, ensuring that patrons would feel as if the theater was exactly as it had been intended in 1880. For example, while the theater features state-of-the-art technology, all of the new audio-visual and heating-cooling equipment have been blended into the structure in order to maintain authenticity. (Below, courtesy of Heidi Gumula, DBVW Architects.)

After nearly 30 years of vacancy, the first performance in the newly restored theater was a production of Prokofiev's *Peter and the Wolf*, which incorporated multimedia additions not possible in the theater's former incarnation. The theater stage had not been used since the early 1980s but, prior to that point of its life, it was the site of many amateur and professional productions, including traveling shows from New York, Boston, Philadelphia, and other cultural centers. Orson Welles, Olivia de Havilland, Tallulah Bankhead, Will Rogers, and Eva Gabor are some of the actors who have graced the stage of the Casino Theatre. (Above, courtesy of John Corbett; left, courtesy of Kim Fuller Photography.)

Above, Tom Pettitt (left), inducted into the International Tennis Hall of Fame & Museum in 1982, was a world champion of court tennis, who also spent some time as a lawn tennis professional in Newport. Pettitt immigrated to Boston from England at age 17, where he proceeded to claim victories until he won the World Championship over George Lambert in 1885. Charles Saunders, right, became the world champion upon Pettitt's retirement from the sport in 1890. The best of the best in court tennis played at Newport over the years and continue to do so in tournaments, such as the Wharton, Pell, and Schochet Cups.

SCHOCHET CUP

UNITED STATES 1973 *PRO SINGLES*

SCHOCHET CUP

2003

United States Professional
Singles Court Tennis
Championships

June 1–8

THE NATIONAL TENNIS CLUB
NEWPORT, RHODE ISLAND

As there are fewer than 50 court tennis courts in the world, the court at the Newport Casino is host to the top tournaments and players. The Schochet Cup, held at the end of May, pits the top 24 players in the world against one another in singles competition, while the Pell Cup, held in August, is an international doubles event, shown below. The court tennis court at the Newport Casino has seen nearly continuous use since 1880 and is one of the few courts in the world open to the public. The unique features of the court—"penthouses," "galleries," and the chase marks on the court surface—are the same now as when King Henry VIII of England played the game. (Below, courtesy of William Burgin.)

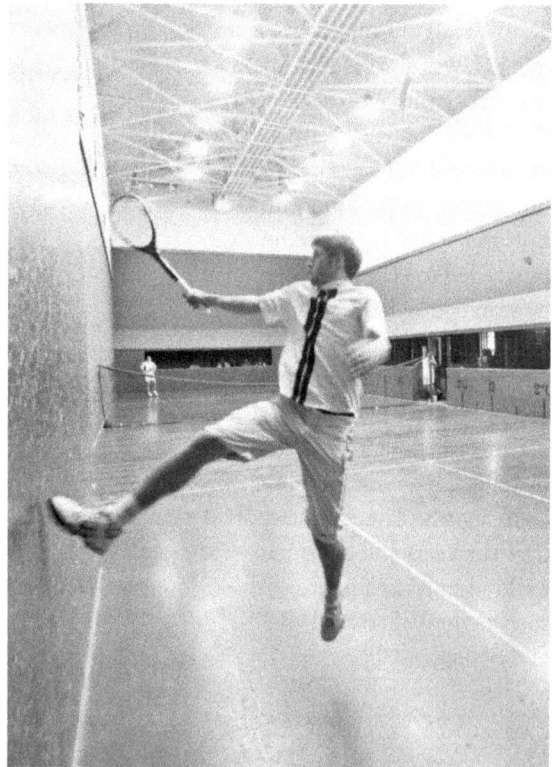

6

SPECIAL EVENTS

The Newport Casino has always served as a center for a variety of activities. The International Tennis Hall of Fame & Museum continues this tradition by playing host to tennis, musical, and star-studded events that have made the Newport Casino such an integral part of Newport's history.

In addition to staging the U.S. Nationals, Casino Invitational, and Hall of Fame Tennis Championships, the Newport Casino has also had the honor of hosting Davis Cup ties in 1921 and 1991. The former tie marked Japan's historic win over Australia to reach the Challenge Round in its first year competing in the Davis Cup competition.

The International Tennis Hall of Fame & Museum also provides entertainment in conjunction with the tennis. Family Weekend is held during the qualifying rounds of the Hall of Fame Tennis Championships and provides families the opportunity to see top-flight tennis and participate in a multitude of tennis-themed activities. During the US Open, the Hall of Fame hosts the Legends Ball in New York City. Celebrities such as Whoopi Goldberg, Katie Couric, Barbara Walters, and others often attend this gala, the Hall of Fame's largest annual fundraising event.

Music continues to play a part in the Casino's history as well. In 1954 and from 1988 through today, it has hosted the opening night of the annual Newport Jazz Festival, where Ella Fitzgerald, Billie Holiday, Ray Charles, and Harry Connick Jr. have performed. It has also served as one of the venues for the Newport Folk Festival, where legend Bob Dylan played, and has hosted the opening night of that event since 2005.

One of the most heart-warming traditions at the Newport Casino is the annual reading of *'Twas the Night before Christmas* by Clement C. Moore, a summer resident of Newport. Jimmy Van Alen, known as "the man who loved Christmas," started this tradition that continues through today. Local children delight in the telling of this fabled tale and are all smiles when the day concludes with a visit from St. Nick.

Truly, the Newport Casino has been and will always be a destination for diverse audiences 365 days a year.

This program is from the 1921 Davis Cup competition. The two-man Japanese team of Ichiya Kumagai and Zenzo Shimizu defeated the Australian team of Clarence Todd, John Hawkes, and James Anderson 4-1 to advance to the Challenge Round. Though Japan lost to the United States at the final hurdle, it proved a stellar Davis Cup debut for the Pacific nation.

This program is from the 1991 Davis Cup tie in which the United States and Spain faced off to reach the semifinals. The American team of Brad Gilbert, Rick Leach, John McEnroe (class of 1999), and Jim Pugh defeated the Spanish team of Tomas Carbonell, Sergio Casal, Emilio Sánchez, and Francisco Clavet to advance.

Tennis is not the only sport played at the Casino. Croquet is also a popular pastime, and the Hall of Fame has the Croquet Club, which is active from May to October. The Horseshoe Court is often transformed into a croquet lawn over the course of the summer, and the image here depicts one of the Croquet Club's members after she just struck her ball toward the next wicket.

The Bill Talbert Center Court is the scene of high quality professional tennis every July, as well as the home of the annual Induction Ceremony. Every August, however, it also serves as the site for the opening night of the Newport Jazz Festival. The Bill Talbert Center Court is packed with spectators who have come to hear some of the greatest names in jazz perform.

Rosemary Clooney was a highly accomplished singer and actress in her own right who spent more than 50 years performing for the public. She is seen here performing at the 1993 Jazz Festival.

Ranked number 10 on *Rolling Stone's* "100 Greatest Artists of All Time," groundbreaking artist Ray Charles was a musical genius able to blend many different styles and make them his own. A pioneer in soul music and other jazz elements, he is pictured here performing as the headliner act at the 1995 Newport Jazz Festival. (Courtesy of John Corbett.)

Tony Bennett continues to thrill audiences with his melodious voice, much as he did when his career first began in the 1950s. Adding jazz singing to his repertoire early in his professional career, he went on to have many hit performances, including one at the 2002 Newport Jazz Festival. Four years later, he was named a Jazz Master by the National Endowment for the Arts. (Courtesy of Kathryn Whitney Lucey.)

Festival organizers would have been hard pressed to find a more appropriate opening act for the 50th anniversary of the Newport Jazz Festival than Harry Connick Jr., who is seen here performing at the 2004 event. Connick Jr. has earned 10 No. 1 US jazz albums, which is the largest number in American jazz chart history. (Courtesy of Kathryn Whitney Lucey.)

When people hear Steve Martin's name, they will often think of his days on *Saturday Night Live* or any of his numerous comedy films. But Martin is also a very accomplished banjo player, and he brought his act to Newport, as Martin and the Steep Canyon Rangers performed during the 2010 Newport Folk Festival. (Courtesy of Craig Harris.)

SPECIAL EVENTS

Two iconic figures to come out of the 1960s were Bob Dylan and Joan Baez. Dylan and Baez are pictured here performing a duet at the 1963 Newport Folk Festival. The performance marked Dylan's first time on the Newport stage. He returned to play the Newport Folk Festival the following two years. His performance in 1965 is where he "went electric." Dylan's decision to go electric is still considered to be one of the most controversial moments in music history. (Courtesy of Rowland Scherman/Hulton Archive/Getty Images.)

Jimmy and Candy Van Alen are shown reading *A Visit from St. Nicholas*, better known as '*Twas the Night before Christmas*, by Clement C. Moore, to children. The Van Alens would reenact the reading of the cherished poem every holiday season, and Jimmy even wrote an extra verse. In keeping with tradition, the Van Alen version of the poem is read to local children every holiday season at the museum.

One of the great traditions at the Newport Casino is the annual Family Weekend, which is held in conjunction with the qualifying tournament of the Campbell's Hall of Fame Tennis Championships. There are many activities for children to participate in, with the highlight being the grass court tennis clinics. Children are seen here at play on the Horseshoe Court during the 2009 Family Weekend. (Photograph by Cailin Mateleska.)

Iconic news correspondent Katie Couric, who became the first female to solo anchor a weekday evening news program on one of the three main American broadcasting networks, shares a laugh with tennis legends Chris Evert and Billie Jean King (class of 1987) at the 1995 Legends Ball in New York. Chris Evert was inducted into the International Tennis Hall of Fame & Museum earlier that summer.

Happily smiling for the camera are, from left to right, Australians Roy Emerson (class of 1982) and Ken Rosewall, as well as Brazilian Hall of Famer Maria Bueno (class of 1978). They are waiting to go on stage where they will be honored at the 1999 Legends Ball.

Posing at the 2007 Legends Ball are, from left to right, Guillermo Vilas (class of 1991); Arantxa Sánchez-Vicario (class of 2007); Hall of Fame president Tony Trabert; the 2007 Eugene L. Scott Award recipient, Andre Agassi (class of 2011); Pam Shriver (class of 2002); and Stan Smith (class of 1987). Sánchez-Vicario, who was inducted that year, won 14 Grand Slam championships. (Photograph by Patrick McMullen.)

Shown at the 2009 Legends Ball are, from left to right, Robin Roberts, coanchor of ABC' s *Good Morning America*; Whoopi Goldberg; Jeanne Moutoussamy-Ashe; and Polly Scott. The late Arthur Ashe (class of 1987) and his widow, Jeanne Moutoussamy-Ashe, were presented with the Eugene L. Scott Award that year. (Photograph by Jennifer Pottheiser.)

7

TENNIS IN THE

MODERN ERA

When the last Newport Casino Invitational Tournament was contested in 1967, the lawns of the Newport Casino began serving as the venue for smaller men's and women's professional tournaments as it struggled to find its niche in the new era of open tennis. It was not until 1976 that it staged the first men's Hall of Fame Tennis Championships, ensuring that world-class tennis would still continue to be played at the birthplace of American tournament tennis.

Today, the annual Hall of Fame Tennis Championships remain the only grass court event in North America played on the men's ATP World Tour. Many of the game's most notable stars have opted to test their grass court prowess in Newport, using the tournament as a springboard to launch highly successful careers. Hall of Famers such as Arthur Ashe, Stan Smith, and John McEnroe have played in Newport. Australian Hall of Famers Mark Woodforde, Patrick Rafter, and Todd Woodbridge played for top honors in Newport, as have other famous faces such as former world-ranked No. 1 Lleyton Hewitt, the record-setting Bryan brothers, and Andy Murray, the most successful male British player of the Open era.

The women also enjoyed their time on the fabled lawns, as the Newport Casino served as a stop on the groundbreaking Virginia Slims Tour from 1971 to 1974 and 1983 to 1990 and as an invitational event from 1991 to 1998. Legends from Margaret Court and Billie Jean King to Chris Evert, Martina Navratilova, Jana Novotna, Pam Shriver, and Arantxa Sánchez-Vicario awed audiences fortunate enough to be holding a ticket to one of the premiere events on the women's Virginia Slims Tour.

From 2007 to 2009, even the Champions Tour for retired professional players saw fit to include a stop in Newport, allowing its competitors such as Champions Tour cofounder Jim Courier, along with fan favorites John McEnroe, Pat Cash, Mats Wilander, and others, the opportunity to compete on the oldest, continuously used competition grass courts in the world.

It is evident that the Newport Casino has seen many tournament formats and competitors over the years, and it is clear that it has and will continue to have a special place in the sport of tennis.

Richard "Pancho" Gonzales always wore his emotions on his sleeve and never shied away from giving his opinions. Equally as colorful was International Tennis Hall of Fame & Museum founder Jimmy Van Alen. Van Alen was also one of the great innovators of the game, and it was his idea of the VASSS (Van Alen Streamlined Scoring System) that paved the way to the modern-day tiebreak. Using the VASSS proved difficult at times for some players, as evidenced by Gonzales arguing with Van Alen over the course of a match that used the new scoring system. The incident became an instant iconic moment in the Newport Casino's history, and a cartoon of the moment seen at left ran in the local newspapers that same week on July 10, 1965. (Below, courtesy of Paule Loring.)

India's Vijay Amritraj was the most accomplished of a set of three brothers who proved instrumental in putting Indian tennis on the map. He won the inaugural Hall of Fame Tennis Championships by defeating American Brian Teacher in the final 6-3, 4-6, 6-3, 6-1 in 1976. He would go on to win the tournament two more times. (Photograph by Michael Baz.)

Having a spot of fun before the 2009 Campbell's Hall of Fame Tennis Championships got underway were Vijay Amritraj's son Prakash Amritraj and 2002 title winner Taylor Dent, son of former Australian professional Phil Dent. They are seen here tugging on the Van Alen Cup within the ATP World Tour Gallery of the International Tennis Hall of Fame & Museum. (Photograph by Michael Baz.)

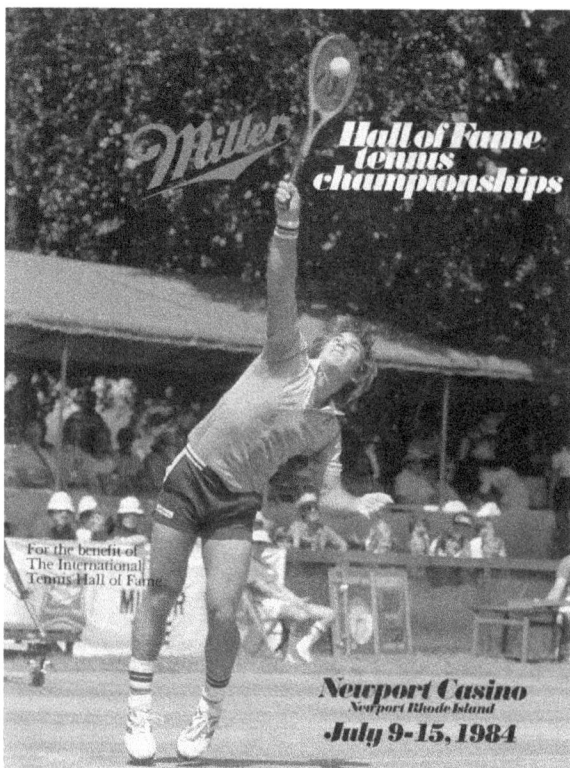

This is a program from the Miller Hall of Fame Tennis Championships. Miller served as the title sponsor from 1976 to 1984. The 1984 staging of the Miller Hall of Fame Tennis Championships saw Vijay Amritraj win his third and final title at the Newport Casino by coming from a set down to defeat local New Englander Tim Mayotte 3-6, 6-4, 6-4.

This program is from the 1986 Volvo Hall of Fame Tennis Championships and features one of the most iconic images of the grounds, with the old-fashioned tennis racquets set off by the one-of-kind Tiffany clock of the Newport Casino in the background. The tournament was won by Bill Scanlon over Danie Visser 7-5, 6-4.

TENNIS IN THE MODERN ERA

Known simply as "the Woodies," Australians Mark Woodforde (left) and Todd Woodbridge (both class of 2010) formed the second most successful doubles partnership in tennis history. In addition to holding Australia's Davis Cup record for Best Doubles Team with 14 wins against 2 losses, they amassed 11 majors and 60 tour titles overall. (Photographs by Michael Baz.)

Crowds flock from all over the country, and in some cases from all over the world, to see the world-class tennis at the grounds of the Newport Casino. Depicted here, crowds at the 1992 Miller Lite Hall of Fame Tennis Championships pack into the stands to watch the competition on the Bill Talbert Center Court. (Photograph by Michael Baz.)

Patrick Rafter (class of 2006) finishes striking one of his devastating and classic backhand volleys at the 1996 Miller Lite Hall of Fame Tennis Championships. The Australian was known for his superb net skills, and they would take him to back-to-back US Open titles in 1997 and 1998, as well as the No. 1 ranking in 1999. (Photograph by Michael Baz.)

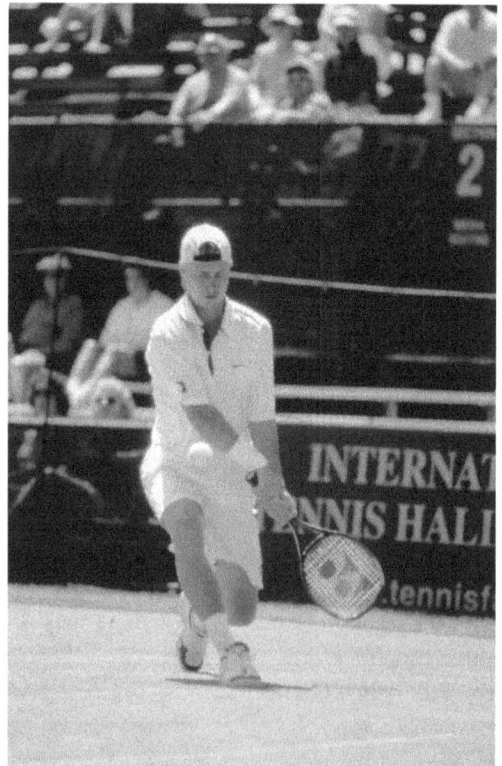

Australian great Lleyton Hewitt prepares to hit his trademark two-handed backhand. He got some of his earliest match experience on the ATP World Tour by playing in Newport. Hewitt went on to win the 2001 US Open, the 2002 Wimbledon Championships, and holds the distinction of being the youngest man to finish as the year-end No. 1 player in the world. (Photograph by of Michael Baz.)

India's Leander Paes finishes hitting one of his textbook backhand slices at the 1999 Miller Lite Hall of Fame Tennis Championships. That groundstroke brought Paes plenty of success in Newport, as he won the doubles title that year with Australian Wayne Arthurs. Paes had won the singles title the previous year over South Africa's Neville Godwin with the loss of just five games in the final. (Photograph by Michael Baz.)

Mike (left) and Bob Bryan are two of the most recognizable faces in tennis and are no strangers to the winner's circle. The American twin tandem broke "the Woodies" record for most doubles titles as a team with their 61st tournament victory in 2010. The twins pose proudly with the trophy after their 2001 Newport win and defended their championship title the following year. (Photograph by Michael Baz.)

James Blake was born in New York, raised in Connecticut, and attended Harvard University so he was always a crowd favorite in Newport. Blake waits to return serve during play at the 2002 Miller Lite Hall of Fame Tennis Championships, which was where he reached the final to face his compatriot Taylor Dent. Dent won the match 6-1, 4-6, 6-4. (Photograph by Michael Baz.)

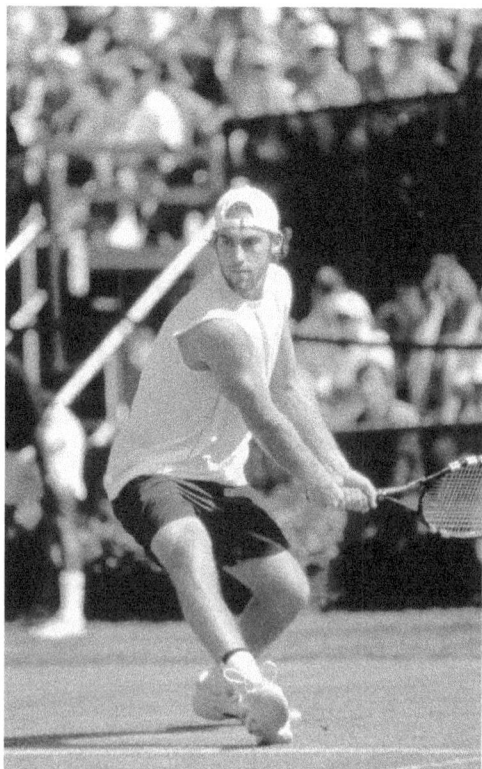

Robby Ginepri is all concentration as he readies to strike his trademark two-handed backhand at the 2003 Miller Lite Hall of Fame Tennis Championships. The American went on to take the singles title that year, dropping only one set in the process. He defeated Austria's Jurgen Melzer 6-4, 6-7(3), 6-1 in the final. (Photograph by Michael Baz.)

TENNIS IN THE MODERN ERA

Greg Rusedski prepares to hit the backhand slice that will help make him the 2004 champion of the Campbell's Hall of Fame Tennis Championships with a 7-6(5), 7-6(2) victory over Alexander Popp in the final. Amazingly, Newport marked the site of Rusedski's very first professional tournament win 11 years prior and also served as the site of his last professional tournament victory in 2005. (Photograph by Michael Baz.)

Young Scot Andy Murray lunges for a low forehand on the grass courts of the Newport Casino during the 2005 Campbell's Hall of Fame Tennis Championships. Murray lost in the round of 16 to France's Antony Dupuis 4-6, 1-6; however, he made a run to the semifinals the following year before losing to American Justin Gimelstob 1-6, 6-7(4). (Photograph by Michael Baz.)

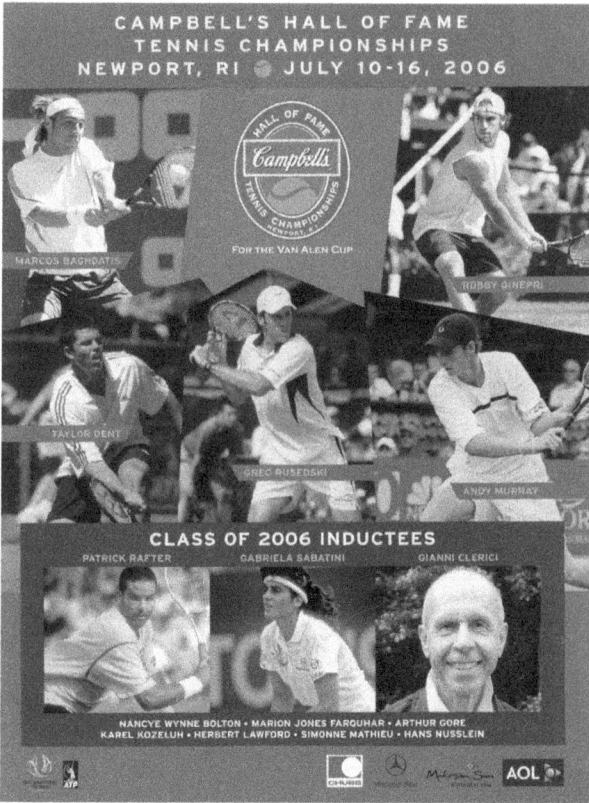

CAMPBELL'S HALL OF FAME
TENNIS CHAMPIONSHIPS
NEWPORT, RI • JULY 10-16, 2006

FOR THE VAN ALEN CUP

MARCOS BAGHDATIS

ROBBY GINEPRI

TAYLOR DENT

GREG RUSEDSKI

ANDY MURRAY

CLASS OF 2006 INDUCTEES

PATRICK RAFTER   GABRIELA SABATINI   GIANNI CLERICI

NANCYE WYNNE BOLTON • MARION JONES FARQUHAR • ARTHUR GORE
KAREL KOZELUH • HERBERT LAWFORD • SIMONNE MATHIEU • HANS NUSSLEIN

Pictured at left is a program from the 2006 Campbell's Hall of Fame Tennis Championships that features such notables as Britons Greg Rusedski and Andy Murray and Americans Taylor Dent and Robby Ginepri, as well as the 2006 Hall of Fame class members Australian Patrick Rafter, Argentine Gabriela Sabatini, and Italian Gianni Clerici. Pictured below are, from left to right, American Justin Gimelstob, Jimmy Van Alen (grandnephew of the International Tennis Hall of Fame & Museum's founder Jimmy Van Alen), and 2006 singles champion Mark Philippoussis of Australia. (Below, photograph by Michael Baz.)

TENNIS IN THE MODERN ERA

Frenchman Fabrice "the Magician" Santoro is all smiles as he poses with the trophy after his 2008 Campbell's Hall of Fame Tennis Championships victory over Prakash Amritraj 6-3, 7-5. In addition to having also won the title in 2007, Santoro holds the distinction of being the only player to have competed professionally in four different decades. (Photograph by Michael Baz.)

Americans Mardy Fish and John Isner celebrate after their 2008 doubles win over the Indian-Pakistani team of Rohan Bopanna and Aisam-Ul-Haq Qureshi 6-4, 7-6(1). Between the Americans' pounding big serves and Isner's imposing six-foot, nine-inch frame, they presented a daunting challenge to every opponent they faced en route to the title. (Photograph by Michael Baz.)

Pictured above are, from left to right, International Tennis Hall of Fame & Museum chairman Chris Clouser; the 2009 singles finalist, Sam Querrey; the 2009 singles and doubles winner, Rajeev Ram; and Jerry S. Buckley, the senior vice president of public affairs of the Campbell Soup Company. Ram made history in Newport that year, as he not only won the doubles event with partner Jordan Kerr, but he also became the first Lucky Loser (a player who loses in qualifying but gains entrance into the main draw through the withdrawal of another player) in history to succeed in winning both the singles and doubles crowns at an ATP World Tour event. Pictured at left, American Sam Querrey was all class as just moments after he had lost the singles final, he thrilled many of the local ball kids by stepping out onto the front lawns for a game of touch football. (Above, photograph by Michael Baz; left, photograph by Cailin Mateleska.)

Olivier Rochus has packed a punch in his two trips to Newport. In his 2009 debut, he reached the semifinals and, in 2010, he went one better, becoming the first Belgian ever to contest the championship match at the Newport Casino. He is seen here competing against American Mardy Fish in the 2010 Campbell's Hall of Fame Tennis Championships. Fish won the match 5-7, 6-3, 6-4. (Photograph by Michael Baz.)

The Virginia Slims Tour, which later evolved into the Women's Tennis Association (WTA) Tour, was founded in September 1970, and the International Tennis Hall of Fame & Museum was among the first venues to offer the women a site to showcase their phenomenal talents. Pictured above, crowds are seen watching the high-quality tennis that was put on display at the 1972 Virginia Slims of Newport event. (Courtesy of the *Newport Daily News*.)

The crowds were treated to seeing some of the best women in the world, as evidenced here where Margaret Court (class of 1979), Billie Jean King, and Jimmy Van Alen are pictured after the conclusion of the 1972 Virginia Slims of Newport women's singles final. Court defeated King 6-4, 6-1. (Courtesy of the *Newport Daily News.*)

After an eight-year hiatus, women's tennis returned to Newport in the form of the Virginia Slims Hall of Fame Classic in 1983. The singles final that year was an all-American affair that saw Alycia Moulton defeat Kim Jones-Shaefer 6-3, 6-2. In the doubles, Barbara Potter and Pam Shriver teamed up to defeat Barbara Jordan and Elizabeth Sayers 6-3, 6-1.

WLKW

PRESENTS

VIRGINIA SLIMS HALL OF FAME CLASSIC

VIRGINIA SLIMS WORLD CHAMPIONSHIP SERIES

JULY 11–17, 1983

Seen here after the conclusion of the 1985 Virginia Slims Hall of Fame Classic are, from left to right, George Graboys, Pam Shriver, Jane Brown, Bud Collins (class of 1994), Chris Evert-Lloyd (class of 1995), Joe Cullman III (class of 1990), and Beth Icoll. Evert-Lloyd defeated Shriver 6-4, 6-1 in the women's singles final. Evert-Lloyd then teamed with Wendy Turnbull to defeat Shriver and her partner Elizabeth Smylie in the doubles final 6-4, 7-6. (Photograph by Michael Baz.)

Shortly after turning professional, American Lindsay Davenport was offered the chance to compete with some of the world's best. She accepted the challenge, and she is seen here competing in the 1994 Virginia Slims Hall of Fame Invitational. While Davenport did not secure the title, the experience helped her go on to have a stellar career that saw her claim four Grand Slam singles titles. (Photograph by Michael Baz.)

Jana Novotna (class of 2005) is a Wimbledon champion and two-time Wimbledon finalist, so she was no stranger to grass. The native of Czechoslovakia is pictured here lunging for a forehand on the grass courts of the Newport Casino as she competes in the 1994 Virginia Slims Hall of Fame Invitational. (Photograph by Michael Baz.)

Jim Courier (class of 2005) is poised to hit a backhand against fellow American Todd Martin as the two competed in the 2007 Outback Champions Series Newport tournament. Jim Courier is the cofounder of the Outback Champions Series for former professional tennis players, and 2007 marked the first of three years in which Newport was included as a stop on the tour. (Photograph by Michael Baz.)

TENNIS IN THE MODERN ERA

8

HALL OF FAME
INDUCTION WEEKEND

In 1955, Oliver Campbell, James Dwight, Richard Sears, Henry Slocum, Bob Wrenn, and Malcolm Whitman took their place in what was then known as the National Lawn Tennis Hall of Fame. Since that inaugural class, the International Tennis Hall of Fame & Museum has inducted more than 200 Hall of Famers from around the globe, and the International Tennis Federation recognized it as the official hall of fame for the sport of tennis in 1986.

Hall of Famers are inducted in one of three categories: recent player, master player, or contributor. To be inducted as a recent player, an individual has to have been either retired or a nonsignificant factor on the ATP World Tour or WTA for at least five years. The candidate must also have a distinguished competitive record at the highest levels of the game and must receive a 75 percent affirmative vote from the Tennis Media Panel, which consists of members of the tennis media throughout the world.

Master player candidates must have been either retired or a nonsignificant factor on the ATP World Tour or WTA for more than 20 years. They, too, should have a distinguished competitive record at the highest levels of the game. Contributors are those who have made significant contributions to the sport of tennis, and retirement is not a requirement for consideration in this category. Both of these categories are voted upon by the International Masters Panel, which consists of tennis media and all living Hall of Famers. Candidates must receive a 75 percent affirmative vote.

In 2010, the International Tennis Hall of Fame & Museum opened its doors to wheelchair tennis players. While these talented athletes are still elected under the three categories listed above, a separate voting panel consisting of individuals knowledgeable about the sport of wheelchair tennis was created.

Today, Hall of Fame Induction Weekend serves as one of the crown jewels in the tennis calendar. Tennis legends such as Bill Tilden, Rod Laver, Martina Navratilova, Stefanie Graf, Pete Sampras, and many more have taken their place in the International Tennis Hall of Fame & Museum during the annual induction ceremony that always marks one of the high points of the Newport summer season.

Members of the International Tennis Hall of Fame & Museum return to Newport for the 50th anniversary celebrations in 2004. Those pictured are, from left to right, (first row) Art Larsen, the Honorable Robert J. Kelleher, Dorothy "Dodo" Cheney, Arthur W. "Bud" Collins, Gene Mako, Vic Seixas, Pancho Segura, Jack Kramer, Frew McMillan, Bob Hewitt, Ann Hayden Jones, Angela Mortimer Barrett, Louise Brough Clapp, Chris Evert, Shirley Fry-Irvin, Rosie Casals, and the Reverend Margaret Smith Court; (second row) Stefan Edberg, Nancy Richey, Hana Mandlikova,

Dennis Ralston, Françoise "Frankie" Dürr, Jan Kodeš, Alex Olmedo, Brian Tobin, Lesley Turner Bowrey, Neale Fraser, Rod Laver, Tony Roche, Lamar Hunt, Maria Bueno, and Virginia Wade; (third row) Tony Trabert, Stan Smith, Dick Savitt, Frank Sedgman, Gardnar Mulloy, Mervyn Rose, John Newcombe, Ashley Cooper, John Edward "Budge" Patty, Roy Emerson, Guillermo Vilas, Nicola Pietrangeli, Fred Stolle, Ken Rosewall, and Malcolm Anderson.

This picture was taken from the top of the south stands surrounding Bill Talbert Center Court during the 2009 Induction Ceremony. The inductees, their families and friends, as well as members of the International Tennis Hall of Fame & Museum Executive Committee are seated on the court, while fans pack into the stands to listen to the acceptance speeches of the new class taking their places among the game's elite. The 2009 inductees included nine-time Grand Slam singles champion Monica Seles, 1972 French Open champion Andrés Gimeno, sports lawyer Donald Dell, and African American tennis pioneer Dr. Robert W. Johnson. (Photograph by Cailin Mateleska.)

In 1931, Briton Fred Perry made the transatlantic trip to compete in the Newport Casino Invitational Tournament as he embarked on the early stages of what would become an accomplished career. Though he lost to Ellsworth Vines in the final, he went on to win the Wimbledon singles title from 1934 to 1936. Perry returned to Newport in 1975 as the first international inductee into the Hall of Fame.

Don Budge and Sarah Palfrey Danzig (class of 1963) clap their hands with the rest of the crowd in recognition of Althea Gibson (class of 1971), who is pictured waving to acknowledge the fans on hand for the 1979 Induction Ceremony. (Photograph by Philip Morris Company/Christopher Morrow.)

Australian Lew Hoad is shown giving a speech during his induction into the International Tennis Hall of Fame & Museum in 1980. He was elected into the master player category for his marvelous career that included four major singles championships, nine major doubles titles between 1953 and 1957, and a prominent role as a member of the Australian Davis Cup team (1953–1956).

Those pictured at the 1985 Enshrinement Ceremony are, from left to right, Jane Brown; Joseph F. Cullman III; class of 1984 inductees Neale Fraser and Manuel Santana; and the class of 1985, which included a family representative for David Gray (who passed away in 1983), Ann Haydon Jones, Fred Stolle, Arthur Ashe, and Bill Talbert.

Fan-favorite Björn Borg of Sweden was unable to be present for his induction in 1987 but came for the 1988 Hall of Fame Weekend. One of the world's most recognized and beloved tennis players, known for his good sportsmanship, Borg won five consecutive Wimbledon gentlemen's singles titles (1976–1980), six French Open men's singles titles (1974–1975, 1978–1981), and represented Sweden in Davis Cup play. (Photograph by Michael Baz.)

England's Virginia Wade (left) is shown here following her induction into the International Tennis Hall of Fame & Museum in 1989 with Pam Shriver. Wade won three Grand Slam singles tournaments over the course of her career and another four in doubles. She has been Great Britain's most successful female tennis player of the Open era. (Photograph by Michael Baz.)

Philippe Chatrier (class of 1992) is shown with Ted Tinling (right), who was just inducted as a contributor into the International Tennis Hall of Fame & Museum in 1986. Chatrier, president of the International Tennis Federation (1977–1991), was responsible for the return of tennis to the Olympics. Tinling was known as the premier tennis fashion designer for such tennis legends as Maria Bueno and Billie Jean King. (Photograph by Michael Baz.)

Though nicknamed "Nasty" for his often-colorful antics and quick temper, Romania's Ilie Nastase proved able to overcome many of his self-inflicted distractions to become a great champion. He won two singles majors and four in doubles by the close of his career. He is giving a speech during the 1991 Induction Ceremony. (Photograph by Michael Baz.)

Tracy Austin (class of 1992) and Pam Shriver (right) play a tug-o-war match over Arthur "Bud" Collins following his 1994 induction. Known for his vibrant personality and wardrobe, Collins is considered one of the most knowledgeable tennis writers. Collins, a well-known commentator and author, was also inducted into the National Sportswriters and Sportscasters Hall of Fame in 2002. (Photograph by Michael Baz.)

Chris Evert and former president George Bush are shown on the Horseshoe Court following her induction in 1995. Evert made it to at least the semifinals for 52 out of the 56 Grand Slam events she participated in, and she holds the record for winning at least one Grand Slam Tournament for 13 consecutive years (1974–1986). (Courtesy of Cullen Designs.)

Perennial fan-favorite Jimmy Connors plays to the crowd during his induction into the International Tennis Hall of Fame & Museum in 1998. Connors holds the distinction of being the only tennis player to have won the US Open on clay, grass, and hard courts. He holds the record for the most men's singles tournament wins at 109. (Photograph by John Corbett.)

John McEnroe is shown here with his father John, mother Kay, and brother Patrick following his induction in 1999. McEnroe won seven singles and 10 doubles Grand Slam titles. He was a Davis Cup team member for nearly three decades before he became team captain in 1999. Today, he is involved in World TeamTennis, sports broadcasting, and playing on the senior tour. (Photograph by Michael Baz.)

Billie Jean King and Martina Navratilova are pictured here following Navratilova's induction in 2000. King won 12 major singles titles and has been an advocate for women's rights. Of Navratilova's 59 Grand Slam titles, a record nine singles came at Wimbledon. Throughout her career, she won 177 doubles titles; her last victory was with mixed doubles partner Bob Bryan in 2006 at the age of 49. (Photograph by Michael Baz.)

Ivan Lendl is shown following his induction into the International Tennis Hall of Fame & Museum in 2001. Lendl was the No. 1 ranked player in the world for four years, winning eight major singles titles (94 career singles titles altogether), and made it to 19 Grand Slam finals. He was also a member of the Czech Davis Cup team (1978–1985). (Photograph by Michael Baz.)

One of the most accomplished tennis players of all time is German tennis player Stefanie Graf. Nicknamed "Fraulein Forehand," she used her favored stroke and slice backhand to devastating effect, winning each of the Grand Slam singles events on no less than four occasions. Her crowning season came in 1988, when she swept all four majors to become just the fifth person in history to achieve the Grand Slam. In Graf's case, it became known as the "Golden Slam," as she won the Olympic gold in Seoul that year as well. Pictured here following her induction ceremony in 2004, Stefanie Graf and husband Andre Agassi pose out front on the Horseshoe Court. (Photograph by Michael Baz.)

Members of the International Tennis Hall of Fame & Museum class of 2005 are, from left to right, Earl "Butch" Buchholz, Yannick Noah, Jana Novotna, and Jim Courier. Buchholz was inducted as a contributor and was a former player and founder of what is now known as the Miami Masters in 1985. Noah was the first Frenchman in 37 years to win the French Open, claiming a singles title in 1983 and doubles title in 1984. Czech player Novotna was the women's singles champion at Wimbledon in 1998 and also has 12 major championships in women's doubles. Courier is a four-time Grand Slam singles champion taking the 1991 and 1992 titles at the Australian Open and the 1992 and 1993 titles on the clay at Stade Roland Garros in Paris. (Photograph by Michael Baz.)

Following an exhibition match during Hall of Fame Weekend in 2007, Rod Laver stands on Bill Talbert Center Court at the Newport Casino with International Tennis Hall of Fame & Museum president Tony Trabert and new inductee Pete Sampras (class of 2007). (Photograph by Michael Baz.)

Tennis photographer Russ Adams is shown on the Horseshoe Court following his 2007 induction as the first photographer ever inducted into a sports hall of fame. Adams, whose career has spanned more than 50 years, was nominated for a Pulitzer Prize in photography in 1955, served as director of photographers for the US Open, developed a "code of conduct" for tennis photographers, and has generated more than 1.6 million sports images. (Photograph by Michael Baz.)

Dr. Robert "Whirlwind" Johnson was a major contributor to the tennis world. A medical doctor by training, but a tennis pioneer at heart, Dr. Johnson, working with the American Tennis Association (ATA), organized a tennis training facility at his home in Lynchburg, Virginia. He was a mentor for many talented African American tennis players, including champions Althea Gibson and Arthur Ashe. He also organized the ATA's Junior Development Program, served as vice president for the ATA, and was named an NAACP Life Membership Chairman. Dr. Johnson, who passed away in 1971, was inducted posthumously in 2009 as a contributor who helped break down the racial barriers in the sport. (Courtesy of the Dr. Robert W. Johnson family.)

Monica Seles (class of 2009) is shown here with a young fan during an autograph and book signing session that took place over Hall of Fame Weekend in 2009. Seles won seven of the eight singles majors she played between 1991 and 1993, collecting nine Grand Slam singles titles altogether and an Olympic silver medal from the 2000 Sydney Games. (Photograph by Cailin Mateleska.)

Brad Parks was inducted into the International Tennis Hall of Fame & Museum in 2010 for his contributions to the founding and development of wheelchair tennis. Confined to a wheelchair following a skiing accident at age 18, he experimented with tennis as a form of physical therapy. Parks founded the National Foundation of Wheelchair Tennis, the Wheelchair Tennis Players Association, and in 1988 started the International Wheelchair Tennis Federation. (Courtesy of Wendy Parks.)

9

MUSEUM

The museum in Newport, Rhode Island, was established in 1954 to complement the newly sanctioned National Lawn Tennis Hall of Fame, later to become the International Tennis Hall of Fame & Museum. From a small collection of trophies and assorted tennis memorabilia displayed on open tables in a few rooms, it has grown into one of the finest sporting museums in the world.

The museum aims to provide visitors with a comprehensive history of tennis from medieval court games through today's high-powered professional sport. Additionally, the museum is dedicated to researching and preserving the history of the Newport Casino, a National Historic Landmark recognized for its graceful McKim, Mead & White architecture and historic grass lawns. The museum, housed in the Newport Casino's main building, encompasses more than 12,000 square feet of interactive exhibits, exciting and informative audio-visual displays, and popular memorabilia of tennis champions past and present, drawing from an ever-growing permanent collection of more than 20,000 objects.

In pursuit of its mission to foster an understanding and appreciation of the sport's impact on our culture, the museum also provides researchers access to a library and archives containing more than 5,000 books, 4,000 videotapes and films, 350,000 photographs, and an extensive collection of programs, magazines, and trade publications.

The significance of the Newport Casino as the site for the museum is not just in its beautiful Stanford White architecture but also in its role as the very place where American tournament tennis began in 1881, when the first U.S. National Championships were hosted on its grass courts. The site still hosts a professional tennis tournament every summer on the oldest continuously used competition grass courts in the world. This unique situation creates an environment in which the building and grounds are as much a part of the museum experience as the gallery exhibits inside.

The museum opened its doors in 1954, primarily due to the persistence of Jimmy Van Alen, who lobbied the United States Lawn Tennis Association (USLTA) to sanction the establishment of a National Tennis Hall of Fame in Newport. Van Alen, shown here in 1961 leading guests into the museum, was a progressive thinker who fervently believed that tennis needed to be willing to make changes in its scoring system. At the Newport Casino, he introduced VASSS, the Van Alen Streamlined Scoring System; electric scoreboards; night tennis; and the tiebreaker, now known as the tiebreak. His original nine-point, "sudden death" tiebreak was implemented at a Grand Slam event for the first time at the 1970 US Open. Van Alen also was a national court tennis singles and doubles champion and remained an active and influential member of the tennis community until his death in 1991. He was inducted into the International Tennis Hall of Fame & Museum as a significant contributor to the sport in 1965.

Uniquely situated on the historic grounds of the first U.S. National Championships in tennis, the museum extends beyond indoor galleries to include views of the grass courts, graceful architecture, and other features of the Newport Casino that shaped the early development of tennis in the United States. A statue of Fred Perry, a member of the class of 1975, commemorates the first non-American to be inducted into the Hall of Fame.

The early 1990s saw a major renovation of the museum floor plan, including the installation of this Grand Staircase, donated by Rosalind P. and Henry G. Walter, which serves as the entrance to the museum galleries. The trophy cases along its rise display prizes won by Hall of Famers from 1884 through the modern era. Other trophies from significant tournaments are on display throughout the museum.

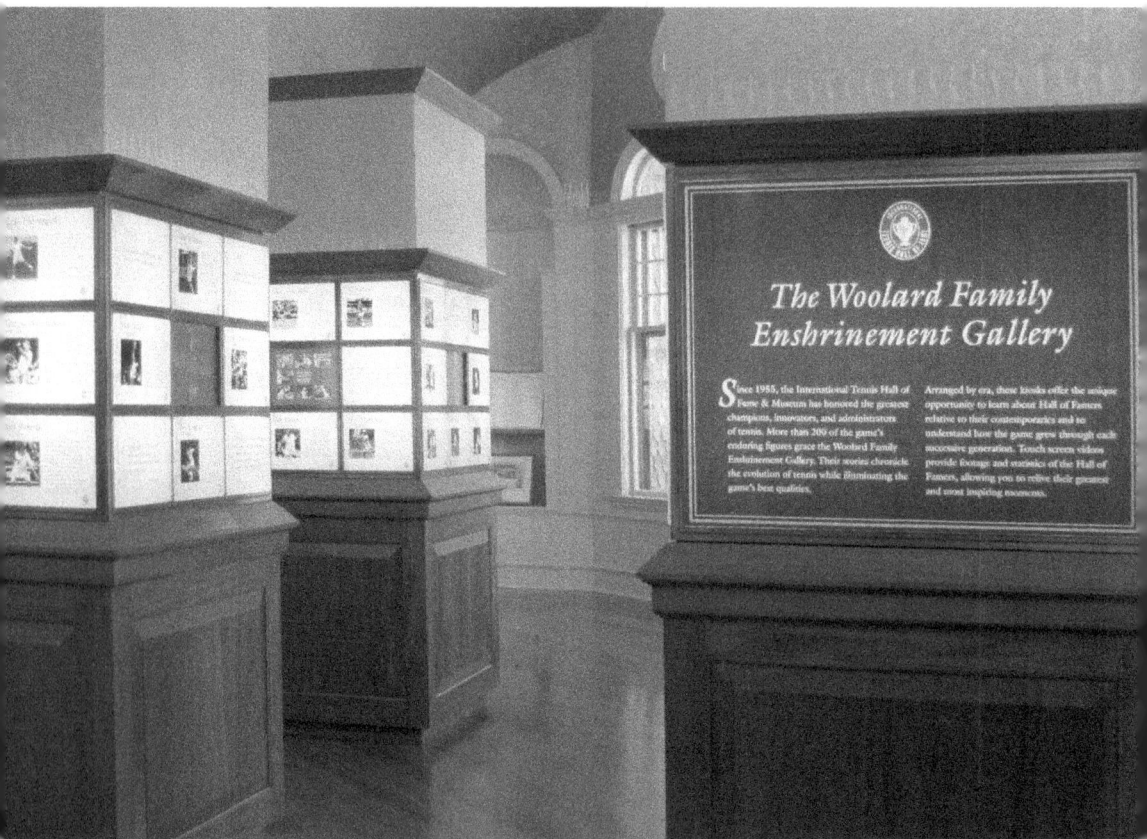

The Woolard Family
Enshrinement Gallery

Since 1955, the International Tennis Hall of
Fame & Museum has honored the greatest
champions, innovators, and administrators
of tennis. More than 200 of the game's
enduring figures grace the Woolard Family
Enshrinement Gallery. Their stories chronicle
the evolution of tennis while illuminating the
game's best qualities.

Arranged by era, these kiosks offer the unique
opportunity to learn about Hall of Famers
relative to their contemporaries and to
understand how the game grew through each
successive generation. Touch screen videos
provide footage and statistics of the Hall of
Famers, allowing you to relive their greatest
and most inspiring moments.

Situated in a vaulted, sunlit chamber that once served as a billiards room for the Newport Casino, the Woolard Family Enshrinement Gallery pays tribute to more than 200 tennis greats inducted into the International Tennis Hall of Fame & Museum. Extensively renovated in 2008, the gallery features interactive audio-visual exhibits at which visitors can call up statistics, photographs, and match footage of individual Hall of Famers. Since the first class of inductees in 1955, the International Tennis Hall of Fame & Museum has honored the game's greatest champions, innovators, and contributors. Honorees have included legends such as Rod Laver, Tony Trabert, Fred Perry, Billie Jean King, and Stan Smith. In recent years, John McEnroe, Stefanie Graf, Martina Navratilova, Patrick Rafter, Pete Sampras, and Monica Seles have been inducted. In 2010, the Hall of Fame inducted Brad Parks, the first wheelchair tennis player, into its ranks.

In addition to being a sporting museum, the International Tennis Hall of Fame & Museum is also dedicated to presenting the history of the Newport Casino, which has been called "the cradle of American tournament tennis" by tennis historian Bud Collins. The galleries of the museum are situated in the same rooms that functioned as a private social club for the leisure-class residents of Newport. The Peggy Woolard Library was painstakingly restored in the mid-1990s with as many original Stanford White–designed furnishings as possible, supplemented with authentic period pieces. The room was designed to be light and airy but take into account cool summer evenings, attested to by the beautiful coal-burning fireplace. This room would be used as a quiet reading or conversation room after a day of lawn tennis. (Courtesy of Greg Premu.)

The museum features many tennis-themed works of art, including paintings, jewelry, sculptures, textiles, and this 19th-century stained glass window, which depicts a woman holding a racquet and ball. The window is believed to have originally come from a spa in the Adirondack Mountains of New York.

Although tennis evolved from many different ball games over the centuries, the modern sport can be traced directly to 1874, when Maj. Walter Clopton Wingfield (class of 1997) was granted a patent for the game of lawn tennis by Britain's Queen Victoria. The game soon became a popular social activity with the leisure class, and the museum displays some of the equipment needed to pursue this early pastime.

Suzanne Lenglen (class of 1978) was one of the dominant players of the early 20th century, along with players such as Bill Tilden, Helen Wills (class of 1959), and the Four Musketeers of France—Jacques Brugnon, Henri Cochet, Jean Borotra, and René Lacoste (all class of 1976). This was an era in which tennis grew dramatically from a casual social activity into a serious sport. Radio and film catapulted players to celebrity status.

The post–World War II years were a time of great change in tennis. Pivotal figures, such as Maureen "Little Mo" Connolly (class of 1968), the first woman Grand Slam winner, and Dr. Robert Johnson, who was mentor and inspiration to hundreds of young African American players, met the challenges of the times and contributed to the betterment of the sport.

Tennis was an Olympic medal sport from the inaugural 1896 Summer Olympic Games until 1924. After only a couple of exhibition years in between, tennis returned permanently to the Olympic Games in 1988. On display are artifacts from these international competitions, including the racquet that Lindsay Davenport used when she won a gold medal at the 1996 Atlanta Games, sportswear from the likes of James Blake and Serena Williams, and the gold medal won by Pam Shriver in 1988.

Alongside Jimmy Connors's (class of 1998) Wilson "T-2000" aluminum racquet, which was used to win the 1983 US Open men's singles title, is the outfit worn by Belgian Kim Clijsters to win her second US Open women's singles title in 2009. This win made her the first unseeded woman to win the US Open and the first mother to win any Grand Slam singles title since Australian Evonne Goolagong Cawley (class of 1988) won Wimbledon in 1980.

Women's sportswear has always been a topic of fascination. The following are just a few examples of shocking fashion choices: Suzanne Lenglen's eschewing the corseted and restrictive dresses of the time, Gussy Moran exposing her lace-trimmed panties at Wimbledon in 1949, and Venus Williams appearing at the 2010 French Open in a black lace dress (right). The museum houses and displays a large collection of tennis fashion, tracing the evolution of individual style in the sport. Notable in the collections are designs by Hall of Famer Ted Tinling (class of 1986), an influential figure in tennis fashion for three decades, from the 1950s through the end of the 1970s.

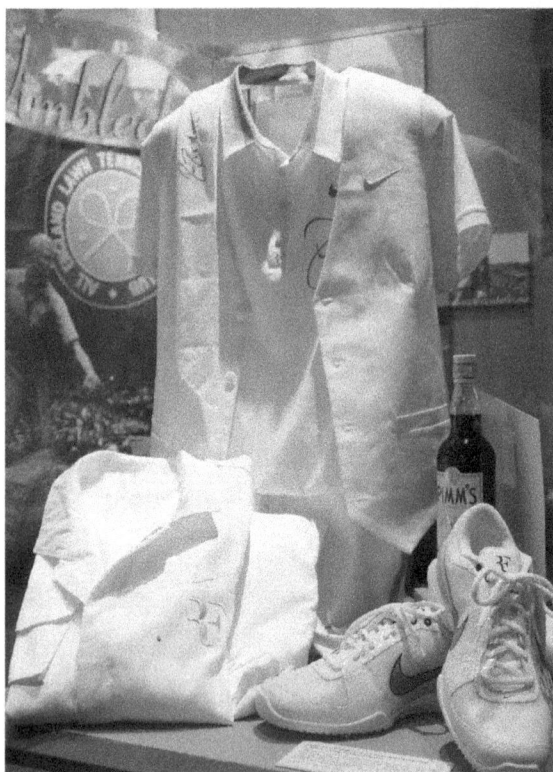

On display are artifacts from the historic 1973 match between Billie Jean King and Bobby Riggs (class of 1967), including King's shoes and Riggs's "Sugar Daddy" warm-up jacket. The match, billed as the "Battle of the Sexes," incited a national discussion over issues such as gender equality, and King, who won the match in straight sets, became a champion of many positive changes for women in sports.

Roger Federer defeated Andy Roddick in a grueling 4-hour, 16-minute match and claimed his sixth Wimbledon title and his 15th Grand Slam singles title, breaking the record previously held by Pete Sampras. On display is the outfit worn by Federer at the 2009 epic match. Memorabilia from many top players are on display in the museum.

Setting records that will likely last a very long time, Frenchman Nicolas Mahut (shown above) and American John Isner competed in a 2010 Wimbledon first-round match that lasted, over the course of three days, 11 hours and 5 minutes. Statistics from the marathon match include 183 games played (138 games in the fifth set alone), 980 points played, and a combined 215 service aces. Mahut and Isner presented memorabilia from the historic match to the museum.

As w
early
the o
tenni
game
playii
press
tennis
yellov
white
for dif
tennis
three

Top or h

Wilso

This ra
of Wor
have lo
when s

Gift of Ir
2003.9.15

TRIO S

This un
way to
can wou

Gift of Ira
2003.9.416

enn "

Tennis Ball used to achieve the Guinness World Record for Longest Rally
...times over 14 hours, 31 minutes by identical twin...

In 2008, twin brothers Angelo and Ettore Rossetti set the Guinness World Record for the longest tennis rally at 25,944 consecutive hits. The record-setting event, which was their second attempt, took 14 hours and 31 minutes to accomplish. The ball on the right was used to set the record, while the ball in the middle is the ball from their first attempt (19,490 hits over 10 hours, 38 minutes).

Educational programs and docent-guided tours are a crucial part of the museum's mission to foster an understanding and appreciation of the cultural and historic links between tennis and society. The museum also offers self-guided audio tours in several languages; hosts numerous events, such as demonstrations, symposiums, and book talks; and provides research services to the public.

The International Tennis Hall of Fame & Museum opened its extensive archival collections to the public in 2000 with the founding of the Information Research Center (IRC). The IRC is open by appointment and contains a plethora of materials that includes a photograph collection of nearly 350,000 still images, an audio-visual collection of approximately 4,000 items, a library collection of 5,000 book and periodical titles, personal collections of Hall of Famers and other important individuals from the sport, and several other archival and reference collections. Researchers from all over the world have utilized this valuable repository of information, and the materials found within the various collections have been used to aide in completing the works of television networks, documentary film producers, authors, magazine publishers, and students, just to name a few.

Visit us at
arcadiapublishing.com

www.ingramcontent.com/pod-product-compliance
Lightning Source LLC
Chambersburg PA
CBHW050601110426

42813CB00008B/2427